Appetite for Addiction

Appetite for Addiction

Spencer Newell

ISBN: 1981896570
ISBN 13: 9781981896578
Library of Congress Control Number: 2017919431
CreateSpace Independent Publishing Platform
North Charleston, South Carolina

I use language in a very direct way; in every culture there are taboo words, and when you use them you're able to interrupt the noise in people's heads. I want to provoke people back into the reality of this moment, that's how they change.

—TONY ROBBINS

Acclaim

"Every day was a 'great adventure.' We'd vanish early with backpacks filled with bread and peanut butter, with bikes and sneakers, drinking from streams, in search of treasure. The gold was fitness and freedom. We were wide-eyed and fifteen, three wiry and invincible best friends. And then the world threw everything at Spence."
—MATT WHITCOMB, HEAD COACH, US WOMEN'S CROSS-COUNTRY SKI TEAM

"Spencer has an incredible story, and I am proud to have witnessed his persistence and resiliency firsthand. We can all learn something about ourselves from the tough lessons he's gone through. His story continues to be one of inspiration, along with being a message of hope and positivity to others."
—WAYNE TINKLE, HEAD COACH, OREGON STATE UNIVERSITY MEN'S BASKETBALL TEAM

"Accepting weaknesses is the first and often hardest step in overcoming them. Since I met Spencer in 2014, he has never been afraid to accept and share his weaknesses or to put in the hard work to overcome them."
—ANDREW MILLER, NORTH FACE GLOBAL TEAM MEMBER / WESTERN STATES 100 MILE ENDURANCE RUN CHAMPION 2016

"As Spencer's endurance coach of five years, I've been side by side with him as he battles his demons and continues to fight the insatiable addictions that send him spiraling into the depths of deep depression and uncertainty. Appetite for Addiction is an unrelenting, honest and insightful journey of a man that gets back on his feet and fights every time this powerful disease knocks him down. This is a must-read not only for those with addiction issues but with Type A personalities and ultra-endurance athletes as well."
— MICHAEL LARSEN, FOUNDER AND HEAD COACH AT LARSEN PERFORMANCE COACHING / 4X IRONMAN FINISHER, NATIONAL LEVEL ROAD CYCLIST

"Spencer Newell's account of his descent into addiction and his victorious emergence from its brutal grip is more than just a memoir: it's an honest, revealing, and often surprising story, at times chilling and by the end inspiring. I'm glad I read it."
— DANIEL OKRENT, AUTHOR OF *LAST CALL: THE RISE AND FALL OF PROHIBITION*, FORMER PUBLIC EDITOR OF THE *NEW YORK TIMES*

Foreword

've known Spencer throughout his story. We were kids together, riding bikes and sneaking out of the house, and we've traveled the country together so many times it's all a blur. One of my favorite memories with Spence was a midnight drive through the most unbelievable Kansas thunderstorm, the likes of which the Northeast could only imagine. The prairie sky was so frighteningly vast and dark, except for the thunderous explosions of lightning, and the soaked highway so drenched that it was as if we were doomed seafarers with nothing left to grip but our mutual sense of adventure. We were young then, equal parts excited and terrified about the night, the trip, and life in general, but we were also innocent, and unbeknownst to us at the time, that storm foreshadowed all that was to come: it marked our one last summer before life really started to beat us up.

Watching Spencer's story unfold was painful and tragic, but at the same time, I've watched him mature in ways unlike that of any other man I know. For so many years, I was the older brother who was most often giving counsel and guidance, but these days, that's been flipped. With everything Spencer has seen, experienced, and felt over these past decades, he has been catapulted into a place of such humble wisdom that he's become an irreplaceable voice of support and often really helps me sort things out and understand them, and he empathizes and sympathizes in a way that almost nobody else in my life can. I'm really hoping that this is what his book can offer to a wide range of people.

You don't need a million friends as much as you really need that **one**. I think a lot of folks have gotten themselves into situations because they didn't have that one person whom they really trusted, the friend who could and would set them straight. I think this book can be that resource for somebody, anybody, all of us. When I'm out of my mind with anxiety or frustration or darkness, it's really nice that I have someone I can call, and what I've noticed from Spencer's online work is that I'm not alone in this; the comments section on his blog has become an impromptu community of people moved by what they have read of his experiences and who are inspired to begin their own journeys publicly and to a warm reception. It seems that there are a lot of us out there who sometimes feel sad or scared or broken, some who have tried to defeat those feelings with methods as equally dangerous as Spence's; but, to a certain extent, anyone can relate to his story. A lot of this is stuff we all have to go through—addiction, maybe, but this is a testament for anyone trying to live in this world who has felt fat or ugly or uncomfortable or angry or out of control, depressed, disappointed, lost. We can all benefit from this raw, honest, patient, and true account of how one person clawed his way out of hell and stays out, day by day.

There's nothing pretentious about this book, and there's nothing contrived. It's just pure thought and emotion, a confessionary, cautionary tale, and a prescription for leaving behind old pains and problems. Spence's way out and how he's been able to make it to the other side and stay there is a loving road map for anyone who needs it. In talking in person with Spencer, there's no judgment, and there's no shame—there's just his persistent desire to understand you and to help you. I think Spencer's openness through his writing is going to affect people the same way. Through that story, that friend, and that openness, those who read this book will feel understood, find understanding, and not feel so alone.

Last time we spoke, Spence told me, "If you want a different life, all you have to do is change one thing."

Oh, yeah, I thought. "What's that?"

"Everything," he said and smiled. What mattered most, though, was that he said it with such confidence—not in himself, but confidence in me: that I believed him. I was inspired to make change. And I believe that this book will do the same for you.

Matt Molyneux
Best friend and writer, guitarist, and singer for the Stickup Boys
Boston, Massachusetts
December 2017

Editor's Note

When Spencer asked me to edit his book, I had no idea how the collective content would affect me. His frequent blog posts on *A Comeback from Addiction, My Story* indicated the subject matter. But when he told the whole story, one page after another, he was creating a message that was stark and raw.

In order to survive the task assigned to me, I had to wear two hats: an objective one that allowed me to do the job I was asked to do and the one where I am his mother.

As his mother, I related to his writing with my heart because he is my son and with curiosity because I communicated with him throughout the entire time he describes—when he was growing up, climbing through an ever-changing web of transitions. I was there on the phone and when he visited home. And I knew nothing about what was going on. Nothing. He told me nothing. And I was suspicious of nothing.

As his editor, I had to suppress my strong maternal instincts and read the words without dwelling on the fact that my son wrote the text I was editing. It was necessary to remove myself emotionally from this nonfictional account and recognize it as a serious story about the struggles of a young person in a grave life-and-death situation.

Spencer's capacity for storytelling and his engaging narrative structure display outstanding creative talent. That he can reveal his own voice to relate the stream of events herein is remarkable to me. That I can recognize that voice invokes wonder and elicits joy.

Lyn Horton
Worthington, Massachusetts
July 2017

Preface

The following recollections come from the combination of memory and third-party accounts. Some of the names have been changed to respect anonymity. The perceptions of people, places, and things are described as how they were at the time and have changed in many regards.

Introduction

August 2007

One hot August afternoon, drunk off my ass after pounding a few tall boys of CAMO XXX malt liquor to comfort me on my drive back to Bend from work, I was late coming home, as usual. I was selling expensive, sought-after real estate with mountain views at a high-end luxury golf resort, about twenty minutes outside of town. That year, I had made it a routine to buy a couple of shitty beers to drink on the way home in order to blow off some steam and lessen anxiety from the work day. My fiancée at the time, Lauren, had left Oregon early to set up our new life in Baltimore, Maryland; my friend Brian was living with me to keep me company. Later that fall, I was planning on heading back east with Brian to join Lauren and complete my overdue exodus from Oregon to the East Coast, which is where I grew up. Oregon had worn me thin, and I was ready to escape.

I drove drunk all the time. That night, I arrived home unscathed, lucky to have not killed myself—or anyone else, for that matter—during the drive. Still drinking potent and fucking awful swamp-water-like beer, I headed for bed, flipped on the television, and tuned in to a *Law & Order: SVU* rerun. Minutes later, Brian entered the house from working all day. He came into my bedroom, saw what was going on, and insisted that I get the hell up and put on my running shoes.

"What the fuck, Brian, leave me alone."

I was hammered enough to forget that I actually had a pair of running shoes. I fought the idea at first, but Brian ended up winning through his persistence. He caught me in a very weak state. Reluctantly, while riding high on the effects of a fabulous buzz, I scavenged up some running clothes, found my shoes buried in the closet, and joined Brian outside just so that he would shut the hell up. I wanted to be left alone to my own devices. I wanted to drink by myself with the shades drawn, in my dark bedroom, in isolation.

After accepting the fact that he was going to force me to run with him, I remember having no pain in my legs and body because I couldn't feel anything other than the tingling sensation of alcohol.

God, I loved that feeling. Being drunk was such a comfortable place. Alcohol in my bloodstream was sinister and dangerous and a real turn-on.

I don't remember speaking a whole lot with Brian while we ran. As we plodded down Parrell Road, the street where I owned an overvalued house in Bend, the guilt and shame of knowing that the past two years of excessive partying, drinking, and drugs were undoing me pervaded my mind. I felt heavy, slow, and fat. Check that: actually, I *was* heavy, slow, and fat. I had gained sixty pounds of body fat over the past two years. I hadn't worked out much since starting my seventy-hour-work-week life peddling high-class golf course property. In fact, every bit of healthy behavior that I had once practiced seemed to have exited my life since starting this job. My idea of health and wellness had to do with the car I drove and the material crap that I had accumulated.

When I finally started running, I struggled for a mile and a half and turned around to head back home. But, maybe due to my buzz or the fact that my legs had warmed up, I started to feel good. Brian and I began to pick up the pace. As we got closer to home, we kept increasing our speed. With around four hundred meters to go, I started to sprint and passed Brian. Although I was drunk, the last few minutes of that run revived a sense of freedom. Maybe I could run? Oh, wait, remember when you were a successful and fit endurance athlete? It seemed like such a distant memory.

A couple of minutes after Brian and I had stopped our jaunt to catch our breath, he said that I had just put down a 23:00 5K.

"Fuck that, dude," I responded.

He reiterated the facts: that I could run; that I still had remnants of fitness in me; and that he was impressed with what I had just done, since the past two years had totally lacked a focus on health. I had sat on my ass making incessant prospecting calls for a living. After all, I was going to be rich!

At the time of his remarks, I didn't hear or believe him. I wasn't ready to take in that kind of encouragement. The only information that registered during that period in my life was how big my bonus check was going to be. I was steeped in an addiction to the allure of money and chasing it. Perhaps Brian was pleading me to reengage in the fit and healthy lifestyle that I had once thrived in—actually, the lifestyle that I had thrived in for the majority of my life up until this potentially revelatory moment. Unfortunately, I was too stubborn and too consumed with my obsession with drugs and alcohol to change myself.

After hitting the shower that night to wash the sweat off, I crawled back into bed, cracked open another beer, and passed out while watching the Oregon Department of Transportation Trip Check channel, the channel that just shows cars going by on select highways in real time across the state, my go-to station when I felt alone and depressed, wallowing in self-pity.

CHAPTER 1

November 2013

Fridays before game days in Corvallis were my favorite. While working at the largest hotel in town, I was privy to all of the pregame action and anticipation for the upcoming football game. The University of Washington Huskies were in town the following day to kick off against the Oregon State University Beavers. My boss, David, and I had scored sideline tickets by way of the Beavers' director of operations under the team's current coach, Mike Riley. The previous two football seasons, largely because of my role as director of sales, I had formed close ties with many of the OSU athletic teams, administrators, coaches, players, and recruits alike. Having that kind of backdoor access to OSU during those years fueled my ego to the fullest. I prided myself on being known in the hard-to-break-into circle of coaches, donors, and athletes. I got used to believing the assumption that I was pretty goddamned important in this college town. It had taken me only a year to gain that status, whereas it might have taken other folks years to accomplish the same position.

Once my duties were tidied up that day before the game, I snuck out the back door of the hotel to start my football weekend. It was my reward for working so hard throughout the week. Plus, due to my sales team's efforts that year, we were crushing our numbers in terms of our budget. So why not leave a little early to get the party started? I deserved it. I always deserved a reward.

This particular weekend was going to be extra rambunctious and predictably careless because I had several friends from Portland and Bend visiting for the game. Filled with excitement about the impending excess that was about to occur, I quickly made my way to the nearest corner market down Western Avenue, just a few blocks away from the hotel. After picking up a couple of potent IPAs, I casually stepped into the invisible, nondescript yard behind the store, where the homeless tended to congregate and sleep, and found a nice patch of lawn overlooking Reser Stadium, home of the OSU Beavers. There I could sit and drink, relishing in how far up the ladder of importance I had climbed in this little college town. Once this train of thought had sufficiently fed my ego, I called some friends to meet them for drinks and continue to soak in my success.

After having drunk myself blind the previous night, I woke up on game-day morning not having a clue where my car was. "Fuck, I must have left it downtown." I threw on my orange-and-black Beavers gear to go retrieve my car and pick up where I had left off the night before with drinking. The enthusiasm continued to build that morning as texts from friends, who were on their way to Corvallis, began to stream in. This was standard operating procedure for most game weekends. Friends plus booze plus football games equaled all the fun. The only way I could process the excitement was to swing by the 7-Eleven and paper bag an IPA on my way downtown to pick up my ride—if I could find it.

Later that afternoon, leading up to kickoff time, I once again found myself clearly overstepping the bounds of intoxication. I had corralled my friends into the parking lot behind my hotel to partake in an hour of pounding Carlo Rossi, the one-gallon red wine jugs that tasted like shit. I vaguely remember who was actually there with me—maybe my friends Rob and Mary? My buddy Cole? Who knows? What I did know was that the gallon of wine that I had in my hand had to absolutely be finished by kickoff, no excuses.

After putting together snippets from friends about my behavior, I can tell the story that once I got to the game, again being on the sidelines with the team, I began to embarrass the hell out of myself. A friend of mine, who is also in recovery, recalls that I was acting like a blithering idiot in front of several OSU donors and administrators, the types who had the status to be on the sidelines. Apparently, I had trouble standing up straight; I had those notorious drunk-leans to the right and left in an effort to maintain my balance. My buddy, whom I did not know at the time, had approached the guy who had originally given me access to the sidelines to ask who the hell I was. My contact's response was something like, "He's just some dude that helps us out at the hotel." I was a pretty important guy, huh?

The evening became worse. I found out later that at the end of the first quarter of the game, I stumbled behind the sidelines and across the field, fortunately keeping out of the field of play, to a set of stairs that led out of the stadium. I had crawled on my hands and knees up the set of stairs next to the OSU marching band, in full view of the entire stadium, to try to make a quick exit, hopefully undetected. It was an epic fail, as I was in plain sight of everyone, including the TV cameras. I'm glad my first appearance on the PAC-12 networks made a splash.

Later that night, I somehow came to in the front seat of my car not knowing how I had gotten there. On top of that, I was in a city park nowhere near where I had left my car before the game. Clearly, I had driven in a blackout to my current location. It was 2:00 a.m. After clearing the fog from my eyes, I noticed that there was still half of a fifth of whiskey sitting in the passenger seat. Being grateful for that, I picked up the bottle, drank the rest of its contents, and proceeded to once again pass out.

Five hours later, I woke up. However, this time I was in my own bed. How the fuck had I gotten home? Fortunately, I didn't have time to assess and replay the evening in my head at that point, because I had places to be.

That Sunday morning my running team and I were scheduled to pose for a photo shoot on and around the trails in Corvallis for a feature in the local visitors' guide. Amazingly, I arrived at the shoot in time, having rustled my shoes and running clothes together. After about an hour of being photographed, the thick haze of my hangover was beginning to fade. I was able to cruise around the trails with my team to capture some iconic shots featuring the lush Corvallis environment. Once we wrapped up the shoot, I returned to my car to prep for the day's prescribed run. With whiskey and wine still flowing in my veins, coupled with shame and embarrassment, I completed a solid twenty-mile trail run up and down the hills of Corvallis, trying to reflect on what the hell had happened the night before. As time progressed during that run, I turned the shame and embarrassment into invincibility and pride. Somehow I could always flip the switch and turn a hangover into a solid athletic feeling. Little did I know what was to come a few months down the road.

January 2014
"I have coke."

That's all that the text message said. The perpetrator, Lisa, who was sitting beside me at the time, was one of the girls whom I had befriended during my dark days because she did not judge me for how I was destroying myself. From my vantage point, she had her own issues with addiction. Whatever, I thought, her shit wasn't my problem. My problem was how fast I could convince her to share the party favors that she possessed.

Lisa and I had met several years earlier while I was living in Bend. When we met, she was immediately adorable in my eyes. I instantly had a crush on her. She had a summertime glow to her that I had often dreamt of when fantasizing about who would be my girl. Unfortunately, the feeling wasn't mutual; she had plenty of other dudes in line, which ruined my chances to be her boyfriend.

One of the guys Lisa was stringing along that summer we met was a fucking egotistic donkey named Jake. I hated him. I was clearly better than he was, so why the hell couldn't she see that? When it was apparent that I wasn't the "one" for her, after only having known her for less than a week, I beat the shit out of myself and mentally kicked the shit out of the other dude she was into. I was the knight in shining armor who could attract *anyone*. Why wasn't my formula of getting girls working this time? Needless to say, regardless of her exploits with other guys, I loved spending time with her, partly because she was attractive and fun to be around, but mainly because she fed my addictions. Not only to drugs and alcohol but to the longing for attention which, of course, was all on her own terms. I was in her control, and I didn't want to let go. I was attracted to toxicity in women, a theme that had persisted with me for years.

Journal Entry

And now there's Lisa. I love her family, her boyfriend cheated on her, and they broke up three months ago. Then she started banging Jake but admitted she had a bit of a crush on me at Colin's wedding this past weekend. She just left town today and headed back to San Francisco. I've been pissed off and bummed all day. Jake was a total fling, and she told him that we made out at the wedding, which definitely fed my ego and gave me some reassurance that she liked me. Matt says to not let her behind the curtain and to not talk about your feelings. I'll just fuck it up if I do. Plus, she's back in town in a few months for Thanksgiving, maybe we can start dating then!

⁂

While staring at the sexy and tempting text she'd sent, I had to make a choice right then and there as to what I'd do next. Whenever cocaine made an appearance in my life, I felt a rush of urgency to jump on the opportunity to snort that shit up. I never knew when the next time would be! And with Lisa being involved, how the hell could I refuse? It was the perfect scenario. I loved the euphoria the drug created; it was just as seductive as the attention I had been seeking from toxic chicks over the last couple of years.

When I read the word *coke* on my illuminated iPhone screen, my synapses began to fire, sparking the excitement for an evening of potential, opportunity, and a big fucking party. I was overcome by the idea that I could get crazy and out of control later that night. Over the last several months, I had been having this experience more and more, confronted with the decision to go for the hit or not. Once my brain became accustomed to the idea that I could get a little extra endorphin boost, there was no turning back. I was addicted to the mere *idea* that I could become something greater, more grandiose, and much more obnoxious and self-deprecating at the same time. At this point in my life, the buzz from booze was starting to lose its glamour; it was boring. I needed something more. I wanted to feel more invincible than I had when I first experienced the effects of alcohol in Worthington, at a buddy's house back when I was fourteen.

After spending all of two minutes debating the choices that were in front of me, I swiftly responded to Lisa: "Guy's room, two minutes." Hell yeah, time to get after it! Lisa and I immediately got up from the table that we were sharing with two other friends and rushed back to the men's bathroom to dive into her shiny plastic baggie of blow. The anticipation of sneaking into a place where we had no business being to indulge in the coke just lit my fuse. After the first line, I overburned my nostrils to get her stuff into my bloodstream; there was clearly no turning back. Oh, my god, I loved this seductive high when I was on coke. Suddenly I felt likeable, attractive, funny, and full of self-confidence, manufactured as it was. It was game on for some less-than-innocent chaos. Maybe tonight would be the night when Lisa finally confessed to me that she was in love with me! This night was starting to look promising.

That evening became a cocaine-and-whiskey induced rampage all over Northwest Portland, OR. Lisa and I had successfully ditched our friends to sneak around the Pearl District to seek out and wreak havoc. I was in heaven. Here I was, with a girl whom I had a massive crush on, running up and down Burnside Avenue looking for more trouble. Cocaine allowed me to really open up with Lisa and be honest and authentic with her about my feelings. In turn, she was telling me all about the guys with whom she had gone overboard. The more she talked, the clearer it became that I was the right one for her. Why the hell couldn't she see this simple fact? In my head, as she talked, I was already planning our wedding.

That night was *supposed* to be low-key. It was early January, and I had come up to Portland to train with my new road-cycling team over the next two days. It was time for OBRA-land (Oregon Bicycle Racing Association) to put the holidays behind and start cranking up the base miles for the upcoming early-season road-cycling races. Two weeks earlier I had returned from the East Coast after spending Christmas in my hometown of Worthington and New Year's Eve in New York City, with a mean hangover, ready to shut the party down for a month to get back in shape. I knew I had gained some weight and lost a bit of fitness during December, so I was anxious to return to training, to say the least.

My standard routine for years was to train my ass off on the bike from January through September, rest in the fall to watch college football, drink beers, find a few more toxic chicks, and check out of my mind for the holidays, only to come back after the first of the year refreshed and ready to start the cycle over again. That formula seemed to work for years, so why couldn't that pattern persist? I had no reason to think otherwise.

This yearly ritual seemed to be working in my favor because I had a boatload of friends from many walks of life and a strong discipline to boot, one in which I took great pride. Everything that I was doing, either drinking or training, seemed to complement the other. Man, I had life figured out. I was unstoppable.

Later that evening in Portland, having temporarily lost Lisa in the chaos of searching for more coke, I found myself hitting a new low. I had stolen Lisa's precious baggie while we were at the Gypsy, a dingy dive bar in the Pearl District, and proceeded to finish the bag that we both had started by myself in one of the bathroom stalls. Unfortunately, my exploits in the men's room, fixing up little bumps of coke on one of my credit cards, leaked to the bartender. As I was cramming the last of the coke up my nose, the bartender busted down the stall door and yelled at me to get out because the cops were en route to arrest my ass. What a fucking asshole, I thought. Who did this guy think he was? He was ruining my fun. My reaction? Run. Hell, four weeks earlier I had just crushed my first fifty-mile trail-running race at the North Face 50-Mile Championships in San Francisco. I thought that I could outrun anybody, including the Portland cops and this overweight pain-in-my-ass bartender.

As I moved strategically from alley to alley, eluding my pursuers on my run from the Gypsy back to my buddy's house on upper Burnside, I remember having several different thoughts go through my head. One, I was fit as hell. Two, I was faster than anyone at 1:00 a.m., even the cops. Three, the Whiskey Bar, an establishment that hosted my beloved rave parties over on First Avenue, was still open. And four, I was fucking hilarious. What a good story this was going to turn out to be! I knew I was going to brag to all of my friends the next day about how bad-ass I had been.

Those thoughts continued to swirl around in my head when I arrived at my buddy's apartment in the early morning. I was so proud of the crazy shit that just went down. It was 3:00 a.m., and I had fled a potentially inescapable situation—yet again—unscathed and ready to brag about it. With that, I grabbed the last few swigs of Crown Royal that were still left in a bottle that I had brought with me the last time I had been in Portland and passed out face first on my buddy's stiff and uncomfortable futon.

Beep. Beep. Beep. Beep.

What the hell is that? I thought as I rolled over on my pillow to the sight of the sun rising over Mount Hood outside of my buddy's apartment window. Damn it, my alarm. Ugh. I had set it yesterday to remind myself that I needed to be downtown at a bike shop at 8:00 a.m. for a group ride with my new cycling team.

While riding downtown to meet the guys, I began to piece together what had gone down just hours beforehand. The timeline in my head didn't seem to make sense. I was consumed by urgency and anxiety, mostly because I had lost my car keys at some point the previous evening. Thankfully I was able to put together a cycling outfit, pound a few shots of espresso, put my bike together, and get out the door with a few minutes to spare. I had escaped another bender. That invincible feeling was beginning to resurface once more.

I arrived at the bike shop for the group ride in a state of delirium, sporting arrogance. I was still drunk and high. Selfishly, I wanted the guys to ask what I had done the night before. The plan for the morning was to get in a good ball-busting training ride. That morning, I turned in a ninety-mile ride around the hills of Portland and the surrounding areas. Not to my surprise, even with the persistent anxiety of wondering where the hell my car keys were, I rode well. In fact, I killed it. My inner monologue that morning said, "Look at me, boys, I bet you can't do what I just did...having the night that I just had. No fucking way, I'm better and more bad-ass than all of you put together. Obviously, you guys are pussies."

As I slowly made my way back up Burnside Avenue to my buddy's apartment, I distinctly remember grooving on this false sense of myself: knowing that I could party that hard on a Friday night, not sleep, and show up to a group ride and still kill it. Throughout the rest of the day, I believed that no one could take away that capacity to be unstoppable. No one could do what I was doing. Once I got back to my buddy's house, I immediately felt like I needed a reward for my accomplishment. Without having even taken off my spandex kit, I dove headfirst into my buddy's liquor cabinet. It seemed to me that he had caught on to what I was doing whenever I was alone in his apartment. He took note that whenever I was visiting, the contents of most of the liquor bottles were mysteriously evaporating, one by one. He was a pharmacist and making good money; he could afford all of the good shit. To avoid being caught again and reprimanded for drinking all of his booze, I fetched my water bottle that I had used on the ride, which still had remnants of Cytomax sports drink in it, and poured a little bit of every single one of his high-end liquors into it, effectively creating the drink that I had coined "the suicide." At that point in my drinking career, it didn't matter how a drink tasted; it was all about what it did for me, my ego, and my mind.

Once I returned to Corvallis at the end of the weekend, what I had just put into the books over the previous two nights gave me an overwhelming sense of confidence. What I was doing was epic, worthy of mention in a Mötley Crüe biography. Epic late nights, epic drugs, epic training rides—I continued to take extreme pride in my ability to live in excess. Apart from the bike rides, I was emulating Nikki Sixx from when he was riding high in the 1980s on the Los Angeles strip. I have always said that if I could go back to any time, I would want to be an eighteen-year-old in 1981, running up and down Hollywood Boulevard, living within the burgeoning '80s hair-metal scene. Perhaps, in my own sick way, I was living out this dream.

Fortunately, the last bit of emotional resolve and sanity that I had kept after getting back home forced me to realize that I had to get straight, go back to work, and put my over-the-top weekend behind me. Throughout that next week, I actually remember having several waves of doubt and guilt rushing through me. I didn't understand their source; I just knew they were there. Maybe I was suffering from the after-effects of a binge, or maybe I felt guilty for jeopardizing my fitness on the bike. One part of me knew the party was slowly coming to an end, yet another small part of me was continuing to reinforce the idea that I truly was invincible. I reluctantly re-dedicated myself to cleaning up my act and getting back into a routine to become fit for the upcoming racing year. I mean, I had to reengage the cycle at some point, right? Plus, all of my race kits didn't seem to be fitting like they used to. Damn it, I was paying for my lapses by gaining weight.

Luckily, the following weekend I was able to douse my bingeing tendency and reset my focus to get in a solid few days of base miles, which led me to believe that I was finally back on track with my training year on the bike. Having gone from out of control one week to in control the next, I was convinced that I had washed myself clean of the recent bad shit I had done. Hopefully I would be able to ride this wave until the following fall, after racing season had ended. Hopefully.

Thursday, February 6, 2014

It doesn't snow very much in Corvallis, maybe once every couple of years. However, this winter, the town was in for a surprise. For the second weekend in a row, I was planning to spend time on my bike saddle to continue logging the base miles. I felt that I had largely reset my body to act as if I were an athlete as opposed to a drunk. Unfortunately, Mother Nature had plans of her own. That Thursday afternoon, it began to snow, harder than I had ever seen it snow in the Willamette Valley. I knew this meant that my biking weekend was going to take a dive because, according to the weather report, the storm was going to cover the area with at least a foot of snow.

As I watched the snow fall from my office at the hotel that afternoon, contemplating how long I would stay at work, I started to wander down a dark path of potential alternate plans. After thinking for about all of two minutes, I quickly shifted my focus and made a very conscious and calculated decision. I knew exactly what I was going to do that night instead of getting on my bike.

As soon as work ended, and it was apparent that Corvallis was going to shut down for the next few days because of the impending snow, I left the office and drove straight to the liquor store. I had made up my mind that I had one more epic weekend of isolated partying in me. The weather was my excuse, and liquor was my cure to escape reality. Perhaps I could build in some extra invincibility, just like I had done the previous month in Portland.

That afternoon I recall walking out of Deb's Mixers, a low-end downtown Corvallis liquor store, with a smirk on my face. I was ready to get after it, and no one was going to stop me. I left the store with two giant plastic bags, one filled with several fifths of Crown Royal Whiskey and one filled with Ninkasi twenty-two-ounce IPAs. At that point in the snowstorm, enough snow had fallen where it was forcing everyone to slow down on the roads; most folks were cruising at a meager ten to fifteen miles per hour.

The roads and the conditions looked ideal for me to hide behind my tinted windows, open a bottle of whiskey, and enhance the drive around the snowy landscape with my little buzz. No one was speeding; the cops weren't out, so what the hell? Plus, I was a great buzzed driver. For me, this seemed like the obvious choice to make. I knew I wasn't going to get caught or pulled over.

An hour and a fifth of whiskey later, I arrived at my apartment. I filled up one of my cabinets with liquor and delighted in the idea of an endless opportunity to be high. I was set to begin my weekend. The storm that pounded Corvallis that weekend has become known historically as the Oregon Snow-apocalypse. For me, however, a different kind of apocalypse ensued. My only real conscious intention over those four days was to stay as unconscious as possible.

From what I recall, here's how the weekend went down:

On Thursday night, I began to drink. I remember being excited to have the chance to drink as much as I wanted, how I wanted, when I wanted. All I really remember doing that evening was pounding copious amounts of whiskey, switching back and forth from my TV to gazing at my laptop, fixated on some girl's Facebook page, while watching incessant reruns of *Law & Order: SVU*.

Friday morning, I woke up and looked out the window at all the snow, knowing full well that work at the office was out of the cards. I found the Crown Royal bottle from the night before and finished it in one fell swoop. It was 7:30 a.m. I then proceeded to grab another bottle, flip off the top, and start guzzling as if I were drinking and enjoying a delightful cup of morning coffee. Once I was good and hammered again, numb from the previous night's hangover, I took out my work laptop and began to do my job as a fully functional director of sales, my position at the time: sending out contracts, responding to work e-mails, logging activities, and scheduling future meetings.

Ironically, I even chatted with some of the running athletes I coached about what they should do in light of the winter storm.

Around eleven thirty that morning, after my first fifth of Crown, I took a lunch break and passed out for two hours on my couch. When I woke up that afternoon, I was stoked that I had faked my way through the day so far. I knew that once I got past 4:00 p.m., I was no longer responsible for work-related activities. At 4:00 p.m., the real drinking could begin.

Once the clock turned over to happy hour on the West Coast, I cracked open another bottle of Crown. However, instead of attempting to work, I switched over to my other drug of choice: attracting attention from girls.

With several pints of liquid courage in my system, I began my attention-seeking, ego-fueled fishing expedition, a game I became an expert at playing on my iPhone. I was feeling drunk and lonely, and I knew how to feel better. Enter: the "pile." The "pile" was a group of females whom I had kept in my life over the previous several years for the purpose of fulfilling a need to feel loved and appreciated by the opposite sex. Lisa, Sarah, and Chelsea were among the distinguished few in my elite and exclusive harem of toxic girls.

For the next several hours, these girls and I bantered back and forth in text messages about anything and everything. I remember that it felt good to have well-deserved attention coming my way. I even went so far as to contact someone who was married and whom I had known for a few years; I actually tried to get her to admit that she liked me more than her husband. It was pathetic. But I was drunk, so I really didn't care what I was saying or how it was affecting other people. And that was my Friday night.

Saturday morning didn't look much different outside weather-wise than it had just twenty-four hours before. Instead of having coffee that morning, I again went straight for the Crown Royal; it was once again only 7:30 a.m. Unfortunately, I had run out of Grizzly Wintergreen chewing tobacco the previous night during my text-capade with all of my girlfriends. I needed to run at least one errand that day.

With a water bottle full of whiskey, I made my way out to my car, which was buried under a foot of snow. I brushed the snow off and continued chugging whiskey as I made my way up Highway 99W, toward Corvallis, to the 7-Eleven. Already drunk, I remember walking into the store, noticing all of the Ninkasi in the cooler, taking note that it was past 7:00 a.m., the time when you could buy liquor in the state of Oregon. Instead of only grabbing a log of chewing tobacco, I also picked up a few IPAs for the road home. Why wouldn't I? It seemed like the right idea. By the time I arrived home that morning from my errand, I was already a fifth of whiskey and several IPAs deep into my day. Without missing a beat from the previous day's routine, I gently settled into my red couch and picked up where I had left off the night before with the "pile." That evening, things began to descend into confusion.

By nightfall, I had created a mess with all of the girls that I had been chattering with in my drunken haze. Two of the girls had stopped talking to me altogether earlier that day, clearly fed up with my antics and recklessness. Caring for no one except myself, I continued to poke and prod for more and more attention, even going so far as attempting to text my ex-fiancée, Lauren, to tell her how much I hated her. When that effort failed,

I got angry and decided to symbolically do something about the "pile." So, with a pint of Crown by my side, I wrote down each of the things I hated about each girl on that list. When I finished, I took my iPhone and began to film a ceremonial burning of the evidence to erase these toxic chicks from my life. I could just burn them away. Clearly, this was the solution to help me feel better.

Content with my expulsive actions, I started to dip into the rest of the IPAs in the house and wound up blacked out for the night. Nothing changed on Sunday. I remember feeling very little emotion. All I remember is feeling helpless and tired. I continued to drink just as much as I had the previous two days. To be honest, I have no recollection of any of the day's activities other than just being hammered and numb.

Monday rolled around, and the snow had begun to melt, which meant that Corvallis was once again operational. I woke up that morning actually anxious and enthusiastic about getting to work. I needed a change of scenery at that point, and honestly, the previous three-day bender didn't seem to affect me in any way physically. I actually functioned pretty well that work day, as far as I know. It wasn't until that evening when something began to change.

Once 5:00 p.m. hit that afternoon, I set myself up so that I would go home and simply have a quiet evening by myself. I felt like I needed to process what I had gone through for the last three days; I felt like I needed to remind myself that I could stop drinking if I wanted to. However, my plans quickly changed. One of my buddies texted me while I was on my way home, saying that he and a few others were down at Bombs Away, a bar in downtown Corvallis, having margaritas. Maybe I would just go and say hello, perhaps have a quick cocktail and head back home. And that is exactly what I did. In retrospect, it was a pretty innocent evening. I was laidback with good company making good conversation. I ended up leaving before everyone else. On my way home, with a slight buzz on, I had a moment of clarity. Maybe I could not say no to alcohol.

After the cocktail at Bombs Away, I had not had anything more to drink. In fact, I went to bed relatively early. The next morning, I woke up with an overwhelming sense of anxiety and despair. I was exhausted, depressed, and emotionally bankrupt. I knew that something had to change or else I would do something to really fuck up my life. That morning I knew that I needed to address my problem with alcohol.

The morning of February 11, 2014, became the day that I started to get sober.

CHAPTER 2

Personal Facebook post, July 28, 2014 (five and a half months sober)

Sobriety: My Story

I need to come clean about something. Earlier this year, in February, a rare snowstorm hit Corvallis and pretty much shut the city down. That weekend I had planned a three-day training block on my bike, but because of snow, I was unable to get out, and the last thing I was going to do was spend three hours on a stationary trainer. Instead of training, I hunkered down for three days and drank, a lot, by myself. It turned out to be the straw that broke the camel's back. That Tuesday morning, I woke up hungover, depressed, and emotionally depleted and decided that it was finally time to address my issues with addiction, 100 percent…no more half-assing it.

Attempting sobriety had been a long time coming. I began ramping up my alcoholic/addictive tendencies in 2006, when my life was firmly out of control: financially, emotionally, and professionally. My addiction then, among other things, was Ninkasi Tricerahops Double IPA and Crown Royal Whiskey. I snuck it, most evenings and sometimes mornings, for two years, unbeknown to nearly everyone in my inner circle. Fast-forward nine years, and I had become a professional closet drinker. Add in the fact that I was training my ass off for various ultra-running and road bike races. I actually took pride knowing that I could spend an entire Friday evening partying and then wake up on Saturday and bust out a four-hour run. I remember telling myself that I'm unique, that I can party this hard and train at a high level: look at me, look at me! Well, this turned out to be complete bullshit and was ultimately part of the behavior that led to my sober date, February 11th, 2014.

Why am I coming out about this now? Because I hate keeping secrets. It eats me alive, and partly because of this obsessive thinking, I just need to get it out there. One of the reasons I have spent most of my free time training for endurance sports is that it has helped me keep my sanity. Now, more than ever, this is true. Am I transferring my addiction from alcohol to running and cycling? Damn straight. Why? Because after a long run or long ride, I get to know myself in the purest form, much more than I would after a long binge on alcohol. I'll take it for now. I'm still very new to sobriety, and in no way am I an expert on the subject...and I will never pretend to be.

So far it's been a very humbling experience and very scary at times. I've got a tremendous support system of friends and family, and I am very thankful for this. Rather than obsessing on the future and what will happen five years from now, I think I'm just going to try and enjoy the fact that today, it's sunny in Corvallis, and there are some trails calling my name.

Thanks for listening. — Spencer —

On that July morning before my Facebook post went online, I found myself running through Willamette Park, a vast network of rolling trails and soccer fields on the southern side of Corvallis, adjacent to the Willamette River. Early-morning runs before work were part of my routine then. I loved them.

Since the start of sobriety, these runs gave me a chance to clear my head before the workday and to contemplate what exactly I was attempting by putting down drugs and alcohol. Up until this point, I had not told very many people in my circle of friends what was going on with me. Many knew that I had stopped drinking, but they did not understand why.

During the run that morning, I had an epiphany about my struggles with alcoholism and addiction that I needed and wanted to become public. I could not explain it. Perhaps it was to seek attention? I always loved an opportunity to garner attention. Perhaps it was to expose myself for the fraud that I thought I had become? Perhaps I merely wanted to tell the truth and nothing but the truth. Whatever the reason, I trusted myself, and upon returning home that morning, I calmly sat at my laptop and typed up the preceding post; took two deep breaths; said, "Fuck it"; and pushed that dreaded button on Facebook: *post*.

After posting my confession to my more than fifteen hundred friends on Facebook that morning, I had an odd sense of relief; I had lifted away a load of pressure and anxiety. It was a euphoric feeling, similar to the one I would compare to a shot of Crown or a line of cocaine. How my friends and family would receive this bit of information was uncertain. Parts of me didn't particularly care what the reaction would be, while other parts were looking forward to the attention that I'd most certainly accept. I remember walking into work at the hotel that morning being cloaked simultaneously in both vulnerability and achievement. I could have worn a T-shirt that morning that read "I'm sober," announcing to everyone that I was conquering sobriety and the world at the same time.

It was strange to feel so naked, as if I had just exposed myself to the world. As I sat down in my office that morning to catch up with Amber and Kaitlynn, my sales team coworkers, I was keenly aware of what was happening on my iPhone. While trying to have an impromptu meeting about the impending activities of the day, incessant Facebook notification pings interrupted me, alerting me to responses to the post I had put up that morning. I voraciously fed off of the attention and couldn't help my-self from scrolling through to see what the reaction was to my admission. Needless to say, I didn't get much work done that day. I was too consumed with how people were reacting. By day's end, the post had generated over 380 likes and more than a hundred responses, all filled with love and the reassurance that I must have done the right thing with going public, an affirmation that I longed for. I remember going to bed that night knowing that trusting my gut and telling the world exactly what was on my mind was good. Invincibility embraced me in the same way as it did when I drank.

Back in February of that year, I could never have imagined divulging to the world that I had been a drinker and addict; that action didn't seem logi-cal. Hell, nothing really did at that point. With that post, my life changed forever as I cast myself into the public eye as an alcoholic.

CHAPTER 3

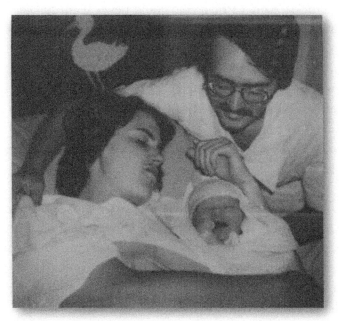

Just a few minutes old on August 7th, 1979

grew up an only child in a remote hill town halfway between Pittsfield and Northampton, off Route 9, in western Massachusetts. My address had always been Harvey Road, Worthington, Massachusetts, 01098. As of today, my mother still lives in the house that I grew up in, which I suppose is something of a rarity these days.

Worthington had, and still maintains, a population of around 1,200, give or take a few seasonal residents. Everyone knew everyone, which could make things interesting personally and politically. It was common knowledge that the local Alcoholics Anonymous meeting was every Monday evening at the church. If there was ever a question as to who couldn't handle his or her booze, all you had to do was cruise past the church parking lot and take a glance at the cars; we all knew who drove what car. And when the local police pulled someone over just past the airstrip off Route 112? Yup. Everyone in town knew about it the next day, mostly due to the chatter of the grocery store cashier, who could never seem to keep other people's business to herself. Needless to say, Worthington was small.

In our one-stoplight town, the intersection of five main streets—known as the "corners"—included the post office (which is in the same building as Corner Grocery Store), the library, and a mysterious historical museum that never seemed to be open. I began to figure that Worthington had no real history to speak of due to lack of interest in that museum. Eventually, we kids would use the adjacent curb as a place to congregate.

Walking distance from our house on Harvey Road to the corners, on Route 112, was exactly a mile. I always remembered that because my mother would take her morning walk to and from our house to Corner Grocery to get the mail, totaling two miles on her feet every single day. Her ambition to stay fit may have actually given me the incentive to become an endurance athlete later on down the road.

Incorporated in 1768, Worthington did, in fact, much to my surprise, have a deep colonial New England history. Tucked within the Berkshire foothills, one of its roads, the Old Post Road, was the historic post road that originally linked Boston and Albany, New York. Worthington was certainly not devoid of its own drama. In fact, the potato farmer, whose fields dominated the town (and who supplied crops for the well-known potato chip company, Stateline) was shut down years ago for several reasons: most notably because he introduced a poison, via an airplane sprayer, to ward off potato beetles, and that insecticide permeated the drinking water in one section of town. The first time I heard the word "dumbass" was in reference to this guy, who happened to be well known as a practicing alcoholic. The potato industry was eventually completely abandoned in Worthington due to his major misstep.

Further south from the corners, down Route 112, was Russell H. Conwell Elementary School, where I attended kindergarten through the fourth grade. Next to the school was the church, which was across the street from the Town Hall. My mischievous friends and I used to break into the church to steal coffee and sugar cubes. We thought we were being bad-asses. I figured I had a free pass anyway because my father was the resident organ player. This section of Worthington also seemed to resemble a "center" of sorts, even though the only commercialism in this area was a massive bed and breakfast that had gone through countless owners over the years. As I remember, every year or so, the rumor would go around town that another affluent family from New York City had bought the restaurant/tavern/bed and breakfast, always promising it would be the last owner. That promise never seemed to come true.

Tapping into my creative side with LEGOs, 1985

Heading west from the stoplight and library, on Buffington Hill Road, past the Okrents' (John Okrent was my first best friend) and the Sharrons' houses, lay Hickory Hill Ski Touring Center, owned and operated by the Sena family as a cross-country skiing facility. The ski lodge building also served as an auction house during the spring and summer months. Most of my later childhood was spent at Hickory Hill, where I would ski on the vast and hilly trail system, bond with my fellow skiers, and forge relationships that I still hold dear to this day. This was the place where I learned about endurance sports. With the trail names still etched firmly in my memory—Bear Hill, Dog's Leg, and Crooked Leg Hill—Hickory Hill remains a subject often for amusement but, more significantly, of personal history, when I think back on how those years indisputably contributed to the development of my training ethic and discipline as an athlete.

When I was in my thirties, visiting home over Christmas one winter, a group of friends and I spent an evening running the overgrown trails in a foot of snow, etching our names on a maple tree at the highest point of the ski area. We wanted to leave a lasting and permanent mark on our old stomping grounds as skiers. It's amazing how much more challenging those trails were to train on when I first experienced them on skis as a pre-teen. It's a shame that Hickory Hill no longer functions as a ski area. Back in the '80s and early '90s, cross-country skiing provided a tremendous outlet for kids to experience the outdoors as opposed to sitting indoors and getting hooked on the trending world of video games. Don't get me wrong, I'd spend hours at the Okrents' playing Tetris; however, skiing became my go-to passion and my purpose. Thank god for Hickory Hill.

Previous to skiing, my athletic endeavors largely included T-ball and Little League baseball at the Rod & Gun Club, down by the West Branch Creek on Dingle Road. I was a Little League pitcher. If I close my eyes to remember, I can still feel the excitement of striking out my first batter, Greg Lenkowski. The emotional vestige of hearing my coach cheering me on after that strikeout still sends chills down my spine. In sports, it was the first time I felt accomplishment.

I would say that baseball was my first love in sports. These days, I continue to be an avid Oakland Athletics fan, largely due to the influence of their esteemed general manager, Billy Beane, the subject of the Hollywood film *Moneyball*. In fact, while visiting Bend for a wedding several years ago, I was lucky enough to meet Billy, his wife, and Scott Hatteberg, a former first baseman for the A's. A friend of mine told me that Billy had bought a place in Bend. She had recently sold him a condo on the Deschutes River. It was a pretty tremendous experience, meeting one of my childhood and present-day idols. The only other idol I had left to meet was Nikki Sixx, the notorious bass player for Mötley Crüe, the leaders in the hair-metal revolution of the early 1980s.

My father knocked it out of the park, so to speak, for me when it came to being an impressionable baseball fan at such an early age. My first experience with Major League Baseball came in the summer of 1988. He had planned a trip to Fenway Park in Boston to see the Red Sox play, and he had the idea to go to the visiting team's hotel before the game in an effort to catch a glimpse of the players. The Oakland A's just happened to be the visiting team! My father had suggested that I carry along some of my A's baseball cards. Freaking genius move on his part.

With a stack full of Oakland A's cards in my hand, I stood with my dad, patiently waiting in the lobby for the players to exit the hotel on their way to Fenway. That morning I met Mark McGwire, José Canseco, Ricky Henderson, Terry Steinbach, Carney Landsford, Dave Stewart, and Reggie Jackson, who was a hitting consultant for the A's at the time. We also had the pleasure of meeting José Canseco's disheveled date from the night before, reeking of booze and sex; she made just as big an impression on me as the players themselves. I still have all of those signed baseball cards, as well as my collection of thirty thousand other cards, which I'd always planned to send my kids to college on. Thanks to my mom for not throwing those out over the years.

Later that night, under the lights of the storied Fenway Park, Mark McGwire crushed two mammoth home runs over the Green Monster.

Having met him earlier in the day, I was awestruck; I had found my favorite player on my favorite team. Later that fall, the A's made it to the World Series, which, unfortunately, was highlighted by the Dodgers' Kirk Gibson limping to the plate in the eleventh inning of game one and launching a Dennis Eckersley slider deep into the right field stands of Dodger Stadium. I remember sitting at home in shock, watching the unthinkable happen to my newly found team. They lost! I was in tears. The pain continued to set in later during that series as the A's got a beatdown and were sent home packing in five games.

Regardless of the outcome in the World Series that year, the A's were, without question, my team. The Bash Brothers, McGwire and Canseco, were my guys. To this day, I get questioned all of the time about why the hell I'm an A's fan, having grown up in western Massachusetts. What can I say? I'm not a Patriots fan either. Go Chiefs! Everyone who questions the decision can blame my dad for bringing me to the visiting team's hotel that memorable morning in Boston. Plus, I got a firsthand look at what a trashy player groupie looked like. Who could deny what an impact that whole experience had on a young and naïve nine-year-old kid? And the KC Chiefs? I don't know...once Bo Jackson got injured when he was with the Los Angeles Raiders, I just started rooting for their main rival. Enter Steve Debergh, Christian Okoye, and Stephon Paige, the core of the Kansas City roster at the time. The rest is history.

Halfway between the Russell H. Conwell Elementary School and the stop-light was the town pool. Each summer my membership was renewed. At noon, when the pool opened, I would bolt down the road on my bike. There I was, learning to socialize as an awkward adolescent. This is the first time I remember distinguishing the difference between girls I liked and those I didn't. I had two favorites during those days, Kate and Lauren. My first full-on crush on any girl was on the lifeguard, Serenity. I can still remember what she looked like in a bathing suit. I was in love.

At the town pool, I began to realize that I might be behind the puberty curve because I began to notice changes in other kids my age—in their voices, their physical builds, and their demeanors. My self-perception of being slow to change informed my awareness at an early age of how I looked and what my voice sounded like. I would obsess about the fact that kids my age started growing leg hair, which is ironic, given that I've shaved my legs for the last fifteen years. These growing insecurities would set the tone for later-life struggles with image and identity. I was behind the curve in more ways than one.

About a quarter of a mile behind the town pool was the Worthington Golf Club. Back then, I always thought that the club was a super-fancy place. Turns out that it was kind of a dump as far as golf courses go. My friend Josh used to wash dishes there. Matt, Matt, and I would always try to distract him and get him to ditch work for some late-night shenanigans. The club was also infamously known around Worthington as the place where the Packards, the Senas, the Jalberts, and the Nugents—all family staples in the community—gathered and dined before heading north on Route 143, toward Berkshire County to the only bar in town, Liston's, where the real party would start.

I heard wild stories about Liston's, like about the time Chucky Baker got into a bar fight or the time when the owner, Steve, eighty-sixed a local snowmobile club. It wasn't until much later in life, around the time I was drinking pretty heavily, that I learned about the core group of drinking buddies in Worthington. It turns out people liked to party in my little hill town. I suppose there wasn't much else to do for entertainment other than get hammered.

My childhood was good. My mother and father raised me well. Sure, I have gripes about some of the things they did, but don't we all? To this day, I have never asked either of them why they didn't have more children.

Being left to my own devices as an only child, with a creative mind that plunged ceaselessly each day into the puzzles that were LEGO Bricks, I was raised to be caring, creative, and self-sufficient, and for better or worse, I became highly sensitive and emotional.

Today, as a thirty-eight-year-old attempting sobriety, I am still uncovering items from my adolescence that had a lasting impact on the person I was to become. Sure, there were scattered incidents that caused trauma, but overall, apart from the occasional argument, I neither witnessed nor was subjected to any physical abuse between or by my parents. Emotionally, though, the dynamic that was created be tween my parents and me as a child still, to this day, exhibits certain characteristics that I resent.

A chilly fall day in my hometown of Worthington, MA, 1982

Like many fathers, mine worked Monday through Friday, at a large regional insurance company outside of Pittsfield. My memory of him was that he wasn't around much when I was a kid, except for on the weekends. Simply put, he worked to keep the household financially stable. My father received a PhD in musical composition; his expertise was in playing the piano and writing music. Only in his spare time could he lean into his creative side. During his retirement, though, in Eastport, Maine, writing, performing, and teaching have become his full-time occupation.

My father always engaged me as a son whenever possible and was a constant supporter of my passion for outdoor sports. We'd play endless matches of badminton, home-run derby, and catch during any free time he had in the afternoons after work and on the weekends. He always was, and still is, extremely supportive of everything I do, both professionally and athletically. I'm not sure he understands what I am engaged in now. Then again, I'm sure many people don't understand the thrill of running one-hundred mile races through the woods!

My mother, like my father, also has the creative gene working in her favor. She is an artist in the purest sense. Her visual art is abstract and impressive yet largely undiscovered. I have always thought that her art would crush it in contemporary markets like Los Angeles or San Francisco. Her fame as an artist is coming; it's just going to take the right person at the right time to figure out that she's an artistic genius.

During my years as a child, my mom stayed at home to watch after me and do her art while my father was at work. She, like my father, was supportive of everything that I set out to do, whether it was a LEGO project, spending time with friends, or my pursuit of Little League baseball. Sure, she said no to things at recognizably appropriate times, like most parents do. But that word was never said in a mean or disrespectful way.

Growing up, I very rarely consciously witnessed my parents drinking alcohol, much less in excess. Therefore, I did not grow up in a household where I was exposed to addictive or abusive behavior, like what many alcoholics experience during their upbringing. As I continue to unravel the roots of my alcoholism, I am amazed that I inherited an addictive personality. In many regards, the pieces don't fit—until I consider my grandparents.

My mother's family, to the best of my knowledge, carries the genetic disposition for alcoholism. My great-grandfather, John Snyder (Poppa), was the secretary of the Treasury under President Harry S. Truman in the late 1940s. Poppa's political involvement set into motion the experiences that my mother had as a child, growing up in a socialite family consumed with image, success, and money in the suburbs of Washington, DC. Poppa was an alcoholic.

My grandmother and grandfather on my mother's side, known to me as Dee and Grumpy, inherited the burden of maintaining the image of wealth that my great-grandfather had imposed on them through his public persona. My grandparents always painted the picture that they had money. Once they moved away from the DC area, they took up residence on one of the barrier islands in South Carolina, which catered to an elite, moneyed crowd. As a child, I vaguely remember the presence of alcohol at their mansion on the beach. In fact, my first taste of alcohol, during one of their many social gatherings, was an accidental swig of a gin and tonic that I had mistaken for a Sprite with lime. It's crazy to think that that instance would be the first of many that would ultimately escalate into a major vice later in my life.

Unknowingly at the time, my first exposure to true and pure addiction came from my mom's sister. I remember hearing descriptions of her addiction in a distant conversation that included words like *drugs, prescription pills,* and *addict.* For all I know, my aunt is still in the grips of her addiction. I couldn't tell you where she currently lives. The last time I saw her was at my grandfather's funeral in the summer of 2006. The so-called wealth that the family had accrued, previous to my grandfather's death, had been significantly diminished, thanks to my aunt. Over the years, she had siphoned hundreds of thousands of dollars from my grandfather's bank account to feed her incessant need for drugs, prescription pills, and love.

My mother suffered from deep depression when I was growing up. Years later, in 2007, I would also be officially diagnosed with the disease. The dynamic that developed between us from her suffering was one that neither of us could have helped. As the only child, without siblings to rely on, I took it upon myself to be the caretaker and to make my mother feel better when she was hit with a depressive wave. I put myself firmly in the cross fire of her disposition. I thought that somehow I was responsible for her emotionalism. With that nagging feeling, I took it upon myself to try to make her happy when things were tough. And when I couldn't, I internalized it and held onto it. Since my mom was the predominant female influence in my formative years, I believe that our dynamic helped set up my constant need for reassurance and female approval. This neediness, in whatever form, can become very addictive.

Setting mother-son boundaries is another challenge that I struggle with, even as an adult. I am befuddled why there weren't more boundaries set between us that could've helped prevent several of my current insecurities. Unfortunately, due to the interaction that began to develop between us early on, our communication can be difficult and memory evoking—and not necessarily in a pleasant way.

When I couldn't help cure my mother, I took it as an indication that I was unlikeable, unattractive, and unworthy to the female sex. Of course, it was not my mother's intention to create the inadequacy I felt. I grew to feel this way because of the absence of my father due to his daily work schedule, my mother's depression, and my being an only child. My awareness that the roots of some of these issues relating to females stem from my childhood enable me to acknowledge and accept that those insecurities around females *do* exist. I will continue to run into these challenges as I move forward as a single male who wants to start a family of his own.

For years, especially when I drank, I would tell myself that I was the victim of growing up with a depressed mother. I may have built up an unconscious resentment toward her. My relationship with my mother will never cease to exist. Crucial to keeping our relationship on an even keel is learning how to communicate effectively, in a way that satisfies both of us, despite our pasts.

As I move forward with an understanding of my younger years, I believe that I have also uncovered the shape of the shame, guilt, and fear that contribute to my vulnerability. I do not place direct blame on my mom for being the way she was and is. If dealing with her was my biggest challenge growing up, I consider myself lucky. Every day I hear stories, especially from those in recovery, of childhood experiences in physically abusive households. I couldn't even begin to imagine such a circumstance.

Now that I understand why I feel vulnerable around women, I can remind myself that the root of that trouble is in the past; it is not the reality of today, because today I am a completely different person than I was then. Living in the past and having anxiety about the future seems to be a constant, especially when my drinking and addiction was at its worst. When I dwell on the past and anticipate the future, I continue to challenge myself. Today I am finding that as long as I accept the fact that I struggle with both psychological tendencies, I can stay in the moment.

My relationships with both of my parents, as I work into years of sobriety, are very much still developing. In many ways, we've only begun the process. I believe that it wasn't until I got sober that I truly understood what having supportive parents meant. In fact, I feel like I am now able to have more candid, honest, and open conversations with each of them individually than I ever did before. When I went public with my struggles with alcoholism and addiction, neither parent really knew how to handle it. I felt that my mother thought that she was in some ways responsible for everything that led up to my difficulties. As for my father, I sensed that he felt helpless and confused, being so far away geographically and not really knowing what he could do. Now that he has a better understanding of my situation, he has become a good sounding board, having accepted my new reality.

In the spring of 2000, during my sophomore year at St. Lawrence University, my parents separated and decided to divorce. This shocked and angered me; I didn't see it coming at all. Unfortunately, this was the first traumatic event that I used as an excuse to drink in excess to numb the pain. Furthermore, at about the same time, I was coming in to my own as a social being at college. By no means was the divorce the only reason for my drinking; it only triggered more heavy drinking, seemingly without consequence. Drinking made everything feel better. I harbored pain because of their divorce for many years. Today I am at peace with it, for the most part, regardless of how either feels about the other. Both have moved on with their own lives. Yes, it was fucking painful at times, but I moved on with them.

Worthington, the 01098, reflects an idyllic innocence to me. Apart from my upbringing, I credit Worthington for offering me a setting to learn about values, adventure, spirit, and discipline. In many ways, I still call Worthington home. I am discovering that the notion of home isn't necessarily a physical place but rather a location established within the heart. The 01098 will always be there, just like our home on Harvey Road. It is important to me, though, to fully embrace and appreciate my "home" on the West Coast, in the tiny college town of Corvallis, nestled in the rolling farmlands between the Cascade Mountains and the Oregon coast. My heart is in this place for a while.

CHAPTER 4

August 2011

Toward the end of summer, I was fresh off a total burnout from road cycling, having all but quit the sport after a rough and embarrassing incident at that year's Cascade Cycling Classic (CCC), a popular race on the Oregon road-cycling circuit. My obsession with cycling had reached an apex. To me, cycling was everything: my identity, my image, my self-confidence. Until it wasn't. Coincidentally, this was also the summer that I met Lisa, and we began what was to become a strange relationship.

Please don't get me wrong—I love the sport of road cycling, and I will buckle down to prep for races from time to time, strictly due to my passion for the sport. How I behaved when I was racing had nothing to do with the sport. Most of what happened to me as a cyclist was purely a consequence of my fragile mental state. I lived and breathed shaved legs, tan lines, and tight spandex. And I was in Bend, which was quickly becoming a mecca for the cycling community.

Around the time that I permanently relocated to central Oregon, Lance Armstrong was already firmly placed on the roster of American sport legends. By that point, he had won four consecutive Tour de France titles. His performance triggered cycling fever in the United States. Not since the days of Greg LeMond, a legend himself, had there been such a heavy stateside interest in the sport. Lance was inspiring all sorts of people to ride and race their bikes. Bend, because of its history of attracting endurance-minded athletes, became a hotbed for road cycling, and I was keen to place myself right in the middle of scene. I wanted to be a part of something, and cycling was it.

From 2008 to 2011, when I took cycling very seriously as an amateur Category 3 racer, I was in the midst of rebuilding myself from the financial and emotional downfall that I suffered in 2006 and 2007 during my involvement with the fact-paced, glamorous game of selling real estate. I traded the addiction of chasing money for the addiction of sport. I was enthralled with my road bike over anything else.

For the most part, immersing myself in the sport of cycling was a healthy activity to keep me in physical shape. Over the years of my association with and exposure to cycling, I forged countless friendships that remain dear to me, even though I am not around the scene as much anymore. By being the team director for the Therapeutic Associates Cycling (TAI) Team, one of the top amateur teams in Oregon at the time, I was able to learn a little about people management, sponsorship solicitation, and managing egos. The positive aspects of this education have benefited me as I move forward in my current job and in athletics. But for every positive, there is also a negative.

One moment stands out in particular. In July of 2011, I led our competitive TAI Cat 3 team (we liked to call ourselves, laughingly, a PRO-CAT 3 Team to satisfy our egos) into the Cascade Cycling Classic stage race, a well-known Pacific Northwest classic. As the team leader, I rallied my teammates to persuade them that we could do some damage in the overall standings. We had a fast group of guys that summer, and I was poised to see myself or a teammate stick it to all the young California punks who would arrive in Oregon to race; I assumed that those racers believed themselves to be top-notch. The CA guys had come to our neighborhood, and it was time for a beatdown from us. We lived here. This was our territory. In those days, I had a blast being the guy behind our strategic approach as a team unit. It bolstered my pride and self-confidence, overshadowing how I really felt about the flaws pervading my arsenal of personal traits. Sending guys off in breaks, bridging gaps, setting tempo, attacking other teams, and taking advantage of other riders' weaknesses tested our modus operandi. Our team tactics did not always work as planned, but when they did, it was extremely satisfying, especially for the team leaders. I used to love it when our team kicked the shit out of other teams and riders.

The first stage of that race was a more than seventy-mile effort with a mean and unrelenting three-mile drag uphill to the finish in the Mount Bachelor parking lot. Our team members had been solid all day, working together, closing gaps, pulling back attacks, and looking out for each other. We did our best to set up our climbing specialists for the last ascent up from Sparks Lake. As we began the final ascent, I settled in midpack to survive with the group. I'm not a natural climber, so I did not want to lose a bucket load of time on the first day. At that point, I was just trying to survive the climb to make it to the next day of the race. Halfway up the hill, another rider crossed his front wheel with my back wheel, which caused my rear derailleur to break, leaving my bike useless. What happened next was a good indicator of where my maturity and emotional instability was at the time. After the "rub," I yelled "FUCK" at the top of my lungs, called the guy who hit me several profanities, and proceeded to throw my multithousand-dollar bike into the woods. I threw a tantrum that a five-year-old would be proud of. It was an incident that I often refer to as an example of genuine childishness. And my reaction after the race was to feel like the victim of someone else's mistake. So, as that victim, I drove down from Mount Bachelor, went to the Circle K convenience store, a shady corner store off of 14th Street in Bend, purchased three Ninkasi Tricerahops Double IPAs, and proceeded to drink all of them, one after the other. Once that beer was in my system, I felt worthy again, having all but forgotten what had happened in the race earlier in the day.

I realize that I was foolish for having reacted the way I did. I had grown accustomed to displaying that type of knee-jerk, immature behavior, not just in cycling but in every part of my life. The rationale for how I acted stemmed from a few things, a bruised ego being the main culprit. For me to not finish that race as the "leader" damaged my ego like nothing else could. I deemed myself weak, unworthy, and a soft cyclist, which is ridiculous, since it was all due to an incident that was out of my control. I had failed at my job, and I took it very seriously and personally.

Cycling was the only thing that I identified with; I was relatively good at it, and with a shot-to-hell self-confidence and ego problem, I took any negative experience or slip-up as a major blow to my self-worth. I prided myself on how fast I was in time trials and how aggressive I was in road races. It was everything to me. And when things didn't go right, my loss of identity drove me to the best medicine to soothe my pain: alcohol. It was a vicious cycle of addictions.

At the conclusion of the CCC, having finished up another road race on Sunday and with an injured ego pulsing through me, I went on a self-induced, one-month all-out bender. Alcohol, cocaine, prescription pills, downers—anything that I could use to empty my mind. Luckily for me, I was able to direct this aggressive substance abuse to prepare for a single event. Just like training for a race, building volume and tapering, I built my alcohol tolerance to an all-time high in only a couple of weeks. Mötley Crüe was on tour that summer and they were coming to Clark County Amphitheater, a short distance from Vancouver, Washington, about a three-hour drive north of Bend. I was ready to dive into an outrage.

The concert weekend was shaping up to be fucking raucous, raunchy, and epic. The day of the show, a group of friends and I drove up to Portland in the early afternoon to get it on early enough to make the event as "motley" as possible. We were on a mission to self-destruct while our favorite band played the soundtrack. I was going to live out another dream of sorts, a party with my all-time favorite metal band.

During the drive north to Portland from Bend, without any food in my stomach, I chugged a few Four Lokos, a disgusting, alcohol-filled version of Red Bull, as well as ingested a variety of mystery speed pills that I had stolen from a friend earlier in the day. Arriving at the hotel in Portland, I was feeling really good, buzzed, and primed to ramp the party up even further. After we checked into our room, our group promptly scurried to the hotel bar, the point at which my memories start to become fuzzy and surreal.

I had yet to eat anything. Our group of four quickly lined up a dozen shots of Jack Daniels and proceeded to toss them all back, not giving a fuck about how much we'd already consumed that day. The more "motley" we were, the better. It must have only been 4:00 p.m. or so, and I was completely shit-faced and incoherent. After exploiting what the bar had to offer, our group boarded a bus that was driving a bunch of folks to the show at the amphitheater just north of Vancouver. Desperately needing a second wind, I took another handful of stolen speed pills on the bus ride, knowing that I might have gone too far too early in the day. I had been through this many times before when my head seemed separate from my body. Inside I felt euphoric, tingly, excited. But my brain was spinning out of control.

I vaguely remember reaching the show. The lineup for the evening began with some local metal band followed by Poison and then the Crüe. After the combination of the local opening band and countless eight-dollar twenty-ounce Coors Lights, I blacked out. I had finally gone over the edge. According to my friends, I was still kicking ass when Poison was on stage, singing along to every single word of their smash hits "Fallen Angel," "Nothin' but a Good Time," and "Talk Dirty to Me." Aggressive fist pumping dominated the action at '80s metal concerts. In that atmosphere, with that number of substances in me, I tended to not give one single fuck as to what I was doing. It was heaven. One clear memory was briefly becoming conscious while leaning against a random tour bus after a security guard had escorted me and a friend out of the arena. What the fuck is going on? I thought. I was puzzled and nauseous and drunk as hell, barely able to hold myself up. It turned out that I had been asked to leave the arena because I was too intoxicated. "Are you fucking serious?" No one tells me what to do at a Crüe show! Whose call was it to kick me out of a Mötley Crüe show? I was going to have words with somebody. It was just a matter of who that poor son of a bitch was!

Somehow, miraculously, after being kicked out, I got back on the actual bus that had taken us to the show in the first place. I have no clue how I got there. Nothing made sense. It was reassuring that all of my friends who accompanied me were on the bus as well. It was illogical to think that we'd all end up in the same place, considering how fucked up we all were. Confused and dumbstruck, I eased my way into another blackout.

Later in the evening, I awoke in bed at our hotel, still dressed in my concert attire, trying to find comfort and safety in the fact that I was not dead. Part of me *wanted* to die; I felt rancid and awful. It was midnight. I had accidentally lost the last four hours of my life. Fortunately, my friends, knowing that I still had not eaten that day, brought back a bag of Taco Bell food to the hotel to nurse me back to health. What a godsend. Chalupas and Gorditas never tasted so good. My friends had been having a blast without me, had seen the show, and had continued to party in my absence. I felt a little jealous knowing that I had missed out.

After the Taco Bell feast, things got murky again. Next up in the sequence of events, my friend Laura randomly showed up at the hotel to stay and help remedy my destroyed body. After she appeared, I blacked out again.

The next morning, I woke up in a total drunken haze. I was in a completely different hotel room, with Laura by my side, when our group of friends from Bend busted in saying that we had to leave immediately to stay on schedule; one of them had to be at work later in the day. I couldn't move. I couldn't even think. I told them to leave without me; they effectively stranded me in Portland. I felt sick, and all I wanted was to be on the cold hotel bathroom floor with a toilet beside me. Resting my head on cold linoleum soothed me.

Once I was forced to check out of the hotel, after requesting two different late check-outs, Laura loaded me up in her car for a tumultuously bumpy ride to her apartment. I had to make her stop a few times on the ride so that I could poke my head outside of the car to vomit. Later that afternoon, after a short and pukey nap, I woke up in Laura's apartment, snuggled up in a blanket on her couch. It was heaven, if heaven meant being hungover and sick with a bucket by my side to catch any of the spew that was still coming out of my body. The rest of that day was spent doing intervals back and forth from the couch to the bathroom. No pill or any type of booze, or anything for that matter, was going to help me get through this period of pain, sickness, and withdrawal. At this point, time was my biggest ally.

Ultimately, I ended up catching a bus back to Bend the following day. That ride was absolute hell. My two-day hangover continued in full force. The end of that bus trip culminated with my running into the bathroom at the bus stop to throw up once more. Safely home, the remedy for my sickness was clear. Go to the nearest 7-Eleven, purchase three CAMO XXX malt liquors, drink accordingly, and get "well." With liquor in hand and plenty already in my system, I blacked out again. It was the only way to cap off a motley fucking weekend.

CHAPTER 5

The town of Worthington, in no uncertain terms, shaped my life. A learning trajectory began there that carried me into my teens. Most kids' hometowns affect them that way, I suppose. There was something about small-town living that invested in me a cohesive set of morals and values that would prove useful later down the road. Sure, Corners Grocery, the town pool, and Hickory Hill Ski Touring Center contributed to my social experience. However, on a spring day in 1992, at age thirteen, my life changed with one phone call. Enter Matt Whitcomb and Matt Molyneux, my soon-to-be lifelong best friends.

That spring day I was at my friend Wayne's house, playing and imitating WWF wrestling superstars, as we did on a weekly basis. I was always the Ultimate Warrior. Wayne usually took the role of Sid Justice or the Undertaker, two of the most popular wrestlers at the time. We would spend mornings watching reruns of *SummerSlam* and *WrestleMania* (premier WWF events) so that we could refresh our moves to practice on each other in our homemade wrestling ring during the afternoons. I remember Wayne's mom calling us to come inside because my mother had called their house to say that she was coming to pick me up early for some reason. I was perplexed, and a little annoyed, that she was taking me away from my friend. Even at an early age I dearly valued any friendships I had developed on my own.

On the drive back to our house, less than a mile away, she told me that Matt and Matt had stopped by on their bikes earlier in the day to see if I was home. I was mildly surprised because I had not had contact with them for what seemed like years. She had told the boys that I was at Wayne's house and that she would go pick me up so that I could hang out with them. I didn't really understand. However, her incredible foresight changed my life. Perhaps she saw a potential protégé-ship with the boys that I needed in my young life. When I arrived home, Matt and Matt were hanging out in our front yard, patiently waiting for me to join them on their bikes for an afternoon of adventures. Happily I quickly changed clothes, grabbed my bike, and headed off with them from my house down Harvey Road. That afternoon marked a significant life change that influenced the next twenty-two years. I didn't realize that I had just adopted two big brothers.

Matt and Matt were both older than me by one and two years, respectively. Due to that fact, I automatically looked up to them and sought their guidance as their naïve little wingman. For years, I felt as though I simply tagged along like an annoying sibling when we'd engage in training for cross-country skiing, go on "SEAL team" (we called ourselves SEAL Team Sixx, in honor of Nikki) missions around Worthington and frequent the Berkshire Mall, all of us acting like normal teenagers. It wasn't until much later in life that I found out that I wasn't, in fact, a mere tagalong but rather a student of their dedication, persistence, desire, and commitment to do in life what they are made to do. Don't get me wrong—they weren't saints. In fact, each had a devious side that I also learned to emulate, for better or for worse.

⚬∞⚬

Matt Whitcomb is currently the head women's coach for the US Ski Team, and Matt Molyneux is a teacher at a private school outside of Boston. Both are total bad-asses in their own right. The lesson I have learned from watching their career paths take shape is one that I've just recently come to respect unquestionably: they exercise a distinct passion for what they do. Studying how they proceed in the world hasn't been a bad thing. At all.

Today, when I look at the relationship among the three of us, one aspect in particular indicates these relationships are for the long haul. Partaking of alcohol or drugs or even entertaining the idea of feeding addictions were never required, nor were they a precursor, in our interactions as teenagers, college kids, or adults. In fact, these actions were so far down the totem pole of our priorities that they don't even register in my mind when I think about relating to the guys over the years.

When time allows, the three of us convene in what we have come to call "summit meetings." These meetings are spent talking about everything in life that we are dealing with, covering the spectrum from money to athletics, jobs, relationships, family, mental and physical health, and, most importantly, the adventures we have yet to embark on in our future as friends. Rarely during these discussions does the subject of alcohol or partying come up. Realizing that fact tells me that the truly important things in my life have nothing to do with my struggle with alcohol, which is all the more reason for me to try to maintain my sobriety. Yes, the three of us have had some pretty damn fun times while drinking; that's the truth. However, if I reflect on the top ten experiences and memories of M2S (our other group tag name), none of them have anything to do with drinking. I would like to continue to hold on to that fact.

Talking with Matt Whitcomb on the phone is a rarity due to his busy work and travel schedule. (If I can, I try to call Matt Molyneux every day because our schedules coincide.) In fact, when I call Whitcomb and the phone rings, I don't even know what country he's in. The last time we had a conversation, he quoted a passage that someone had sent to him the week prior: "The goal in life is to live young, have fun, and arrive at your final destination as late as possible with a smile on your face, because this would mean that you truly enjoyed the ride." Those words, coming from a best friend whom I've looked up to and admired, really struck a profound chord with me. And I have taken those blessed words inside of me.

The bond that Matt, Matt, and I shared had partially to do with our insatiable thirst for adventure and pushing the limits of our parents' patience. One summer day in late August of 1995, the three of us had an experience together that collectively changed our idea of what it meant to feel alive. This was a day for the record books.

Reluctantly, my parents allowed me to climb into the car with Matt and Matt to leave Worthington together for our first road trip. Molyneux had just received his driver's license. The destination that afternoon was SPAC (Saratoga Performing Arts Center), a three-hour drive away, to go hear Tom Petty, one of our favorite artists, play in concert. Being with my two best friends on our first road trip, without parents, was a total thrill.

Together with my lifelong best friends, Matt and Matt,
rocking out before a Mötley Crüe show, 2001

Much to our dismay, we had arrived at the concert a full week late. This became glaringly apparent when we arrived at the ticket booth requesting tickets for that night's show. The agent said, "Great, have you ever seen *Jesus*

Christ Superstar?" Uh, what? No, we came here to see Tom Petty. "Is *Jesus Christ Superstar* opening for Tom Petty?" Matt asked. Our first attempt at a road trip turned sideways; we were left to our own devices in the SPAC parking lot. Oddly, the mishap turned into opportunity.

It was 4:00 in the afternoon, and I had an 11:00 p.m. curfew back in Worthington, one that I could not ignore since I was given the first chance to be with my friends. If I screwed this one up, I knew I'd be grounded for the rest of the summer. On our way back to the car with our heads down and our minds working overtime, Matt threw out an unlikely suggestion: "Let's go catch the sunset on top of Mount Washington." Without hesitation or concern, we climbed back into our van and took off toward northern New Hampshire. I had no idea where we were going or just how far Mount Washington was from our current location in upstate New York; all I knew was that at some point I was going to have to find a pay phone and let my parents know where I was.

After doing the math, I knew damn well that there was no way we'd be back by 11:00 p.m. This was new territory for me. I had broken the rules in Worthington before, staying out past curfew, roaming the country roads late at night on my mountain bike, but this was different. I was in a different state, hours away from where I was supposed to be. I was the youngest of the three, so I figured that my say really didn't matter. My impending doom was on its way, courtesy of my soon-to-be furious mother.

The dynamic among the three of us, from my perspective, has always been that I am under my guys' wings. Countless times, around some of our older friends whom Matt and Matt admired, I felt inferior and self-conscious. It sucked. It was the first time that I truly felt worthless and intimidated in the presence of my friends. Since they had become my two surrogate older brothers, I immediately thought that I had to play by their rules and let them lead. I just had to go with the flow, which led to some timeless memories. Even with the pain of the inferiority complex that crept up on occasion when I was around them, I am still grateful that they influenced me in their own unique way; they each had something that I wanted. Both were and are athletic, attractive, amenable to girls, funny, confident, and well liked. These characteristics were foreign to me as a prepubescent teen. I looked up to them without hesitation, hoping that if I stayed close to them long enough, perhaps I could become like both of them.

From an athletic standpoint, both of the Matts were extremely accomplished junior cross-country ski racers. Both trained their asses off all summer and fall to get ready for the upcoming winter race season, year in and year out. When we were preteens, Molyneux was the fastest. I put him on a pedestal during my time as a junior ski racer. He had the coolest sunglasses, the best equipment, and the most sought-after race suits. I always loved ski race suits for some reason. I still have every race suit that I've worn since 1994 somewhere in storage, and I'll never throw them away.

Matt Whitcomb was not too far behind him in talent. In fact, as time went on, Whitcomb became the fastest of all of us on skis. Being just a year younger than Molyneux, Matt took a while to catch up. When he did, mostly because of Molyneux's new obsession with following the Grateful Dead instead of training, Whitcomb never looked back. Within a couple of years, he climbed to the top of the ranks for New England high school cross-country skiers. Because of their early involvement in the sport, coupled with the fact that I had the highest regard for both of them, cross-country skiing became *my* new athletic passion, replacing baseball. I wanted to be as good as the two Matts were. The success they had was very appealing to me. Being driven by the idea of wanting to get faster because they were faster, I could not think of a better sport to get into, as it is potentially one of the most difficult sports in the world to excel at, especially from an endurance perspective.

As we negotiated our way through central Vermont and New Hampshire that evening, a term was coined that would forever change our lives. While on the remote and windy Kancamagus Highway, about an hour from Mount Washington, I found myself drawing a map of our journey thus far on the roof of the van with a whittled-down piece of white chalk. As I retraced our path, I sat back and declared to the boys that we were on a "great adventure." Little did we know that the spirit of those two words, of that idea—the great adventure—would lead us to places later in life that would ultimately shape us in unimaginable ways.

Much to no one's surprise, we completely missed the sunset on Mount Washington. I think Matt and Matt knew what they were doing all along. I always assumed they had a plan up their sleeve to keep pushing the boundaries of what was acceptable to our parents. At this point, we were too far into our journey to consider even turning back to go home to Worthington. In a way, we had broken free of the reins with which our families in Worthington held us back. It was at that moment that I started to get really frightened of how my mother was going to react to our ignoring the conditions for leaving town together. For some reason, breaking the "rules" felt good, like I was growing up to some degree. I was on a road trip with my two older brothers; nothing could prohibit us from totally kicking ass on this adventure.

"Wanna go see Maggie and Chris?"

Norway, Maine, was the home of the two hottest girls on the New England junior cross-country ski circuit, the Shaner sisters. Molyneux was dating Chris at the time. Whitcomb had been keen to follow suit within the family because he had been working up to a thing with Maggie. We were only two hours away. It quickly became clear that we'd continue our journey east into our fifth state of the day. Again, I had no say in the matter. When the Shaner girls were on the line, I just had to shut up and go with it. Later that evening when we arrived at Chris and Maggie's house, it was right around the time that my parents expected me home. I had no choice; I had to make the phone call. This was going to be a first. I was fucked.

"Fucking Molyneux!" my mom yelled at the phone. "How the hell did you end up in Maine?" This conversation was heading south quickly.

My bullshit and obscene excuse had something to do with the car breaking down and our having to hitchhike to the next town. Of course, none of it made a lick of sense. It was the most unbelievable story I had ever told, a complete lie, and my mother did not buy it. Nor should she have. I never had witnessed her being so pissed off at me or at a situation. The lasting picture of that scene, with all of us as witnesses to the havoc occurring over the phone, was Molyneux finding cover under the kitchen table with his hands over his ears, trying not to hear my irate mother screaming through the phone handset. I knew there was absolutely no way in hell that she'd ever let me go on another road trip with Matt and Matt again.

The agreement that I made with Mom in the phone call was that we would hit the road back to Worthington as soon as the sun rose. I fell asleep that night on a fold-out couch with Whitcomb next to me (he didn't close the deal with Maggie that night) in awe of how the hell I had gotten to Maine. I was amazed at what had happened; the event was simultaneously thrilling, terrifying, and satisfying. I wanted more.

On the trip home the next morning, I reveled in how lucky I had been to acquire such cool and adventurous friends. While on this trip, I had realized I was no longer an only child. Matt and Matt had opened up a whole new meaning of the word *adventure*, and I was hooked.

Already thinking about our next road trip, we arrived back in Worthington early the next afternoon. Needless to say, my mother was still furious. As soon as I got out of Matt's van after pulling into our driveway, she just told the boys to go home. Promptly and without discussion, I was grounded for the first time in my life. For the rest of the summer until school started, I was not allowed to hang out with either of the Matts. That was devastating. But I knew that we had just forged a bond as brothers that could potentially last a lifetime.

The tradition of the great adventure did indeed live on. In a sense, that spirit of adventure still thrives today, although it has been some time since it has been unlocked in its truest form with the three of us together. After a little convincing, and since I was a year older, my mother let me get into the same car with the boys the next summer for another road trip. This time, however, there was no curfew; we had the freedom to launch out on a road trip with fewer conditions. This summertime tradition lasted a few years until 1998, when we stepped up our game.

In the winter of 1998, in a rundown hotel room in McCall, Idaho, Matt Whitcomb and I reached a decision that together we were going to take summer great-adventure road trips to a new level. We were in Idaho for the Cross-Country Skiing Junior Olympics, an invitational event that brings together the fastest junior skiers in the country. After getting our asses kicked in the fifteen-kilometer classic-style race earlier that day, we brainstormed ideas for how we could ski faster.

Both of us had our sights keenly set on racing for collegiate ski teams at the division-one rank. Our meager results at Ponderosa State Park in McCall that winter did not build the confidence we sought. It was at this point that Matt suggested a little town in Oregon that one of our skiing friends, Tim Woodbury, had moved to the previous summer so that he could train on snow during the summer months. Apparently, Bend played host each summer to many of the Olympic cross-country skiers who were looking to get some time on snow while everyone else in the country was roller-skiing and doing dry-land training. Matt's idea was that we would drive across the country the following summer to join Tim in Bend so that we could get some valuable on-snow training.

Theoretically, the idea sounded great. There was one problem. The following fall I was heading into my freshmen year at St. Lawrence University, and I was positive that my parents wouldn't let me embark on such an adventure, given the big life change that came with the onset of college. I mean,

Oregon? Really? To be honest, I had no idea where Oregon was in relation to the rest of the West Coast. I knew that the idea was so far-fetched that I was scared to bring it up with my mother. Fortunately, after about a week of discussion, my parents and I drew up a contract as to what would happen if Matt and I were to do this. Basically, the contract necessitated that I find a job, have money to eat, and find a place to live. I had no idea how this was going to work; I knew I had to try. Matt was the adventurer-in-chief on this, and I was willing and ready to take a leap of faith with him. I trusted him with every bone in my body, and for some reason, my mother did as well. My guess is that it had to do with his status of being the "Good Matt."

Later that June, Matt and I packed his two-door hatchback, affection- ately known as Aunt Susie, and headed due west on I-90. We were bound for a state on the other side of the country that neither of us knew anything about. The thrill of heading into the unknown was inspiring and exhilarat- ing. Unfortunately, the other Matt (deemed "Bad Matt" after our first great adventure) was not with us for this trip. His cross-country skiing career had simmered down that year because he was busy being a sophomore at Middlebury College as well as trailing the cultish band Phish around the East Coast. Phish had provided an outlet for Deadheads, after the Grateful Dead disbanded upon Jerry Garcia's death. It was beyond me. A self-proclaimed hippie at this point, Molyneux had no interest in moving to a "podunk" town in Oregon to watch Whitcomb and me train on snow all summer.

Although this was not technically a great adventure, as we had come to define it over the last four summers, the trip maintained the great ad- venture's spirit. Without our friend Molyneux, whom we considered a key ingredient, the two of us set out to rewrite our own rule books in support of our motivation to embark on life-changing adventures.

Driving across the United States for the first time was an experience I will never forget. The distance of the drive was beyond comprehension for me.

We were heading into the unknown, away from our families and friends, away from New England, and away from our homes. That first summer in Bend, in 1998, our eyes were opened to a world of new possibilities, landscapes, and lifestyles. Immediately upon our arrival, Bend cast an aura around itself that I was attracted to. This aura existed for years.

Fulfilling the job category, we became housekeepers at a shady chain hotel in south Bend, partly because we thought it would be funny to write Molyneux and tell him what we were doing. We both knew he'd get a laugh out of it. Being the only male housekeepers, in company with fifteen or so young and middle-aged women, we were constantly the butt of their jokes as well as victims of their innocent and incessant harassment.

For food, we would routinely go to McDonald's at first, living on twenty-nine-cent hamburgers. Wednesdays and Sundays were special because they offered thirty-nine-cent cheeseburgers. We stocked up our fridge with those hockey pucks called burgers, along with rice and bean burritos from a taco stand, topped off with cabinet of ramen noodles that we'd devour for dinner.

For a roof over our heads, we found a hole-in-the-wall complex called Aspen Court, located on the fringes of the popular Bend Westside. I was pleased and proud to make the phone call home only four days after arriving in Bend to tell my parents that I had met my side of the agreement. We were making it on our own. And that felt good and empowering.

Matt and I had shared the drive out west with another of Matt's college teammates, Justin Beckwith. After meeting up with Tim Woodbury, the person who helped inspire this journey the winter before, Justin, Matt, and I lived in a two-bedroom apartment that was reminiscent of a dilapidated college dorm room. It was disgusting.

Justin slept in the living room on a couch that we had grabbed from one of the former tenants. Matt and I shared a mattress that we pulled out of the dumpster upon our arrival, and Tim had a blow-up mattress that he slept on. Obviously, Tim was the one living in luxury. We were the definition of poor, vagabond athletes chasing our dreams of becoming elite cross-country skiers.

The daily routine that summer was straightforward and simple. Mornings consisted of some on-snow training at Mount Bachelor among several elite and Olympic cross-country skiers (Pat Weaver, Justin Wadsworth, Ben Husaby, and Beckie Scott, to name a few) who had also migrated to Bend to spend the summer on snow. Being in Bend, Matt and I knew that training here was going to give us a substantial leg up in terms of fitness heading into college. Afternoons were spent at the hotel, making $5.75 an hour cleaning toilets and changing bedsheets, while the evenings were spent trying to convince Tim, who had a killer fake ID at the time, to go over to the Chevron station next door to pick up some beers.

Living in Bend that summer was uplifting, eye-opening, and inspiring in many ways. I was pushed out of my comfort zone and, in the process, fell in love with the mystique of the West Coast. But the fact that Molyneux had not accompanied us meant that the spirit of the brotherhood that we had formed on our drive to Norway, Maine, had splintered. I remember having an uneasy feeling that summer because we had left him behind. I felt a personal withdrawal from him. Fortunately, we would change that circumstance soon. In subsequent years, he would join us on our annual summer trips out west.

The dynamic of having two older brothers to whom I constantly compared myself became more of a challenge as I aged. At first, I was thankful to have such incredible influences so early in my life. However, when I hit my late teens and early twenties, I started to feel that I was less than, slower than, not as cool as, and less attractive than my guys. Something changed for me that didn't quite make sense. Perhaps it was due to the late onset of puberty or that I felt as though I was treated unjustly by them for so many years. I didn't want to be "under their wings" any longer, and I started to rebel against them a bit, which may not have been apparent to them at the time. I also noticed that the two of them began having a relationship that did not seem to include me. They'd have their own jokes, talk about things I wasn't aware of, and engage in activities that would normally include the three of us. I felt rejected, and I actually resented them to a small degree in my early twenties. My own insecurities began to creep up and get in the way of our relationship as best friends.

I remember several summers later, in Bend, a group of friends and I, including Matt and Matt, were hiking up Mount Bachelor, and I had a complete breakdown with my friend Lilith about my relationship with them. I was convinced that I had been living in their shadow for too long, that I was not important, that I needed to step out on my own and distance myself from these two guys that I had looked up to over the years. It was a painful realization. They were family to me, and I was pissed off that I wasn't getting any of their attention. They seemed not to even notice me any longer. In my head I had created the narrative, based mostly on illusion, that I wasn't cool enough, which unfortunately opened the rabbit hole to additional insecurities that ran deep. I dove in with both feet.

Meanwhile, the great adventure lived on. Once Matt and I had seen Bend, we couldn't wait to return home to try to recruit more of our friends to come with us the following summer. For the next three summers, the troop grew from a trio of adventurers to a band of nearly twenty-five friends, not all cross-country skiers, coming from St. Lawrence (my school), Middlebury (Matt and Matt's school), University of New Hampshire, Williams College, University of Vermont, Bates, and Colby. We had successfully converted the great adventure from a simple one-day road trip to Norway, Maine, to a full-on pilgrimage of friends out to the West Coast.

The narrative of Matt, Matt, and me, which had progressed in my head to be a somewhat bitter sibling rivalry, finally boiled over during our last summer in Bend because of a girl, when we were all drunk as hell. The scene unfolded outside of Bend's best-known and most classic dive bar, the Westside Tavern. The three of us spent the evening trying to catch the eye and attention of one of the girls in our entourage. I remember jockeying all night to make sure that I appeared to be the coolest and the best of the three. At that time, I didn't feel worthy around girls without having liquid confidence in the form of alcohol. Ultimately, the game didn't work in my favor. Everyone in our group was hammered that night and keen to take sides once the impending verbal fight between the three of us broke out. Once it was clear that one of the Matts and I weren't going to win the battle over "getting the girl" and the other Matt won, we got out of control. Accusations started flying.

I'm not sure why it all came to a head for me, but the argument began to ramp up in a Zima-fueled haze (leave it to Zima—that Sprite-flavored alcoholic drink had been a staple that summer); I remember telling one of the Matts that I hated and resented both of them for the way I was always treated like the little brother. In response, Molyneux turned to me and the rest of the group and proclaimed that he had "quit" the great adventure. I responded, "Fuck it," and ran off into the night, away from the bar.

For four summers, we had migrated across the country together, a group of ragged college athletes in the midst of an incredible bonding experience, and now we were breaking up over a silly argument about a girl. The irony of the situation was that another buddy of ours, who was also with us that summer, ended up marrying that girl. In my mind there was clearly more at stake; years of emotions had been tied up in my heart, only to be released in one instant. It was awful to feel as though I had disowned my two best friends in the world. But I was drunk and being overly dramatic, so it seemed like the right thing to do then.

That night after I stumbled home, I recall being consoled by someone, sobbing that I had lost my brothers. It was a heartbreaking experience. Ultimately the three of us made up over that night, but what it brought out for me was a lack of self-identity and image. I was proud that I modeled myself after them for most of my life. Call it jealousy or unleashed pride, but I knew that night at the Westside that I needed to become my own person. This set into motion an often silent rebellion against them that lasted for several years and into my late 20s, unbeknown to both of the Matts. I was too afraid to bring it up with either of them.

As time went on and we each got older, it became clear to me that the relationship dynamic that I had imagined, especially as to how I fit into the trio, was mostly an illusion. These days, whenever the three of us get together, it takes about five minutes of awkward adult talk before we click back in to the comfort zone that we created together as kids. Because of Matt Molyneux's regular job as a teacher on the East Coast, my daily phone call to him is one way for us to stay in touch and maintain sanity. With the other Matt, other than an occasional "like" on Facebook, I don't expect to communicate with him much during the ski season. However, he has recently started visiting Bend each May for an on-snow ski camp at Mount Bachelor, which allows me to see him for enough time to share an overview of our lives and the directions we are heading. Of course, I would enjoy spending more time with them both, but life got in our way. That happens.

The last time the three of us were together was in 2015 for the Boston Marathon. Molyneux had been granted entry through a charity program and was excited to tackle his first marathon. Whitcomb and I were lucky enough to meet him at the bottom of the infamous Heartbreak Hill and usher him in to the finish, running by his side all the way to the iconic Boylston Street finish line. The experience meant the world to me: to participate in my new passion of running, with the both of them, in an epic and hallowed setting. The time we spent together for those short few days had everything to do with respecting and celebrating the friendship that the three of us had started almost twenty-five years prior. Matt and Matt are my brothers, my best friends, and my family. It is an honor to call them a part of my team.

CHAPTER 6

Fall 2011

After eight years of hoping, wanting, and obsessing, Sarah and I finally got back in touch. We had originally met at a wedding in 2004. She was a bridesmaid in the wedding party for my friends Chris and Reese. The first time I laid eyes on her I was immediately smitten. Throughout that wedding weekend, I was lured into her mystique and beauty, which was unlike anything I had ever experienced before. Somehow I convinced myself to ask her to dance, which led to spending all night together on a beach, watching an endless stream of cars cross a bridge from Oregon to Washington. That evening was very innocent, and I recall nothing of the conversation. Just being next to her was intoxicating.

Thanks to Facebook, we reconnected. After getting good and drunk one night, I looked her up and requested her friendship. Within minutes, she accepted. I summoned the nerve to send her a message. To my surprise, she responded. Part of me thought that I had come on too strong; the rest of me didn't care. Luckily, Sarah remembered me. Was this too good to be true? Why did I wait so fucking long to do something about her? What a dumbass I was for putting this off! I felt like an innocent little kid who was reaching out to his crush of a lifetime—kind of like when I was a seventh grader passing a note in Mr. Noe's science class to one of my three middle school crushes, who were, ironically, also all named Sarah. Leave it to my obsessive nature to keep the namesake going.

In a twist of fate, it turned out that Lisa and Sarah were from the same town and knew each other, although Sarah was a few years older. What were the chances of that happening? In my tangled world, I suppose there are no surprises, especially with the women I surrounded myself with. I think that Sarah had even babysat Lisa on occasion.

A couple of months later, Sarah and I got reacquainted over coffee one morning in her hometown, the same town where we had spent the evening together years before. I was heading to a cycling race in eastern Oregon, so I figured this would be my opportunity to swing up her way and meet up in person. Other than that, I had no real reason to travel through her town, since Chris and Reese had already moved away. Moments before she showed up, I felt nervous as hell, questions swirling through my head. Would she look the same? Would she immediately walk out? My thoughts were riddled with insecurity.

After several minutes of waiting, thinking she'd blow me off, Sarah casually walked through the door, as seductive as ever. She looked exactly how I remembered her: petite, blond, stunning, gorgeous. I fell in love with her all over again. I was screwed.

After a wonderfully long conversation, save the awkward initial five minutes of small talk, we rekindled a friendship and kept in relatively consistent contact. Fortunately, later in the fall I had another excuse to be in her neighborhood, again for a wedding; I made damn sure I let her know that I was in the area so that I had an excuse to escape the wedding and get into her neck of the woods. We met up for dinner that night in a seedy dive bar. It felt sexy as hell for me. Actually, doing anything with Sarah was sexy as hell. It's the way she made me feel.

After a couple of hours of stiff cranberry-and-vodka cocktails and conversation, Sarah made an off-the-wall and unexpected suggestion. She asked, "Need anything else to keep the night going?" My initial thought was, Don't you know who you're talking to? I coolly responded, "Yeah, I'm game for whatever." Minutes later, I found myself outside with her, in her car, doing Texas-sized lines of cocaine off an old and scratched-up CD that was propped up by her console. The evening had taken a seductive turn for the better. If I was on a nine-out-of-ten high before the trip to her car, after doing some blow with her, I jumped to a solid and robust twelve. Turn that shit up! This was heaven. Cocaine turned me into a superman.

The evening progressed just as it had begun. We ended up back at her house, imbibing gallons of tequila and inhaling loads more blow. This was not a proper recipe for recovery because earlier that morning I had gone on a twenty-two-mile training run. We stayed up all night, talking about life, emotions, feelings, depression, transgressions, athletics, and everything in between. I think I even alluded to the fact that I had had an eight-year crush on her. Finally, around 7:00 a.m., I fell asleep with her curled up next to me on her couch, not really sure of what to make of what just happened.

As time passed, Sarah and I continued our under-the-radar friendship. Many times when I'd return to her hometown to visit, we'd grab a casual beer or cup of coffee so that we could pick up the conversation where we had left off. Conversation with her was so completely natural; there was an unmistakable flow of banter that never seemed to lose its rhythm. After that night of totally rocking out together, we gradually began to see each other more and more, each time repeating the process of getting drunk and high and talking about life. Even with being fucked up, I adored the raw, authentic, and honest dialogue that we shared together. With each instance of being around her, my admiration and affection grew even deeper, to the point where it became dangerous. Enter Jason, her boyfriend. The cover of our underground relationship had been blown, and he was pissed off, rightfully so.

Unfortunately, the development of our relationship was not mutual. I was once again falling for her just as I had done eight years ago. Currently Sarah was in no position to even consider a relationship with me, as she had her own shit to deal with—like being in a dysfunctional relationship with a guy who she had been with for years. With her being unavailable, I became more and more addicted to the idea that she and I should be together. Of course, it made perfect sense for that to be the case. Our relationship had been largely copacetic up to this point. We were having a platonic affair. But I could still feel the wheels falling off for me emotionally. It wasn't necessarily desperation, but the belief that I had finally found "the one" was anxiety inducing. That feeling, coupled with excessive cocaine and alcohol abuse, put me into a complete tailspin.

Journal Entry

I'm fucked up right now, super depressed, and drunk as hell. I cannot stop thinking about Sarah. There is a huge cycle-cross race going on right now, most of my teammates are competing, and all I want to do is sit on the couch, drink, and be depressed. All I want is a partner in life; all I want is Sarah. The only thing I can do right now is nothing, and that kills me. I got used, and it hurts. Remember, the girls in the pile took something from you and gave nothing back. All I want to do is crawl into a hole. I want to be Jason, I want what he has, and there is nothing that I can do about it. I want Sarah, the booze, the drugs, and the love.

Jason sent me an e-mail today accusing me of fucking up his relationship. He's right! I am fucking up their relationship. Matt's advice to me is to just tell myself "fuck that guy." Maybe he's right— fuck that guy! I know their relationship is dog shit anyway.

They are about to go on a trip to Europe together. Let's look at the facts: 1) Sarah is with Jason; 2) they are about to go on a five-week trip all over Europe together; 3) she lives with him; and 4) they've been dating for years. Seriously, dude, this is all of the information you need to know right now. Fuck, I bet he proposes to her on their trip. Look, until she's single, it's time to go away and protect yourself. She said she likes getting e-mails from you, but what is that going to do for you? Nothing, it's all about giving her what she wants, endless attention. All I'd be getting in return is reassurance that I'm likeable. I suppose this is what happens when I act as the replacement boyfriend.

Damn it, I got used! FUCK! I gave Sarah a reason to question her relationship, almost like she was using me for leverage somehow. I fucking told her everything she wanted to hear so that she could feel better. The cocaine, the booze, the euphoria, the dream of it all got wrapped up into one big game, and I lost. I got played! At least she doesn't live in Bend. That would suck.

Can I trust anything that she said to me? Telling her that you were falling for her was probably exactly what she wanted to hear. When are you going to learn that girls with boyfriends are flight risks and not to be fucked with? Have fun in Europe, Sarah. The cocaine, the booze, the dream of being with you was great. Time to let it go, dude.

<hr />

Despite her being in a long-term relationship, as time progressed, our friendship became even more destructive due to substance abuse—more booze, more cocaine, more of whatever we could do together. I believe that Sarah was a major crutch for me in terms of safety because she did not judge me. As I had felt with Lisa, I also felt safe with Sarah to explore and enhance my substance abuse issues to the fullest. My demons were being exercised. The more time we spent together and getting high, the more and more depressed and anxious I felt; I was slowly sinking into a dungeon of despair, looking for her to commit to our relationship because I felt unloved and unworthy. I wanted love from her so badly it hurt. I would do anything to have someone tell me that the feeling was mutual. Especially if that sentiment came directly from Sarah. My journals during that time were front-to-back words describing thoughts and feelings for Sarah, much like they were before about Lisa.

Our friendship culminated a couple of years later when Sarah agreed to come to Corvallis to spend the weekend with me. At this point in my alcoholism, I would do whatever it took to go out of my mind, and I would normally do it on my own. The minute she showed up to my apartment, the coke and tequila started to flow in excess. Once more, I was caught up in some sort of fantasy that here was the girl whom I had longed to be with eternally, in my apartment, hanging out with me. We got totally shit-faced that weekend. It also unlocked the doors to our physical relationship, which just set my love for her over the top. I was living out the dream that I had always wanted, and I didn't want it to end. Ever.

Little did I know that our weekend in Corvallis would be the last time I would see Sarah before I attempted sobriety. After getting sober, the communication with her fell off the rails. We didn't talk at all, which saddened me deeply.

After a couple of years, Sarah and I began to connect once again with each other via occasional text messages. Despite the dark times that we experienced together, the conversations that came up were as memorable, honest, raw, and authentic as they had been originally. Although our life circumstances are different today, I still believe that I have a connection with her both physically and emotionally. I suppose it's really hard to say because we haven't been face-to-face since I cleaned up my act. Seeing her again? A matter of chance and time. Who's to say what my reaction will be with clear eyes. I just hope how we related in the past doesn't get in the way of staying in touch.

CHAPTER 7

n 1995, I was a sophomore at Gateway Regional High School in Huntington, Massachusetts. I had been cross-country skiing competitively for four years, immersed in a western Massachusetts training group led by one of my first mentors and coaches, Ed Hamel. This group of dedicated teenagers deserves its own chapter in my story, but, for now, it simply serves as a precursor to a relatively dramatic change in my life that was about to occur in my high school years.

Matt Whitcomb and Matt Molyneux were both part of Ed's training group, gradually making names for themselves on the New England junior cross-country skiing circuit. Around this time, with the big picture in mind (to prepare for skiing at the division-one level in college), they both took the leap from Worthington to attend one of the most distinguished cross-country ski academies at the time, Stratton Mountain School, located in Stratton, Vermont. Looking up to those two and wanting the same thing, to ski competitively in college, I followed their lead to try to become a faster skier. However, my path would lead me in a different direction—north from Stratton, up Interstate 91, into Vermont's northeast kingdom. Enter Burke Mountain Academy (BMA).

Together at the 1995 Junior 2 New England Ski Championships with Jason Lemieux (left) and my first mentor/coach Ed Hamel (center)

BMA is located three hours north of Northampton, Massachusetts, via the Lyndonville exit on the interstate in East Burke, Vermont. When my parents and I were looking at options as to how to further my development as a skier, we came across BMA as an underdog of sorts in the world of New England's ski academies. Seeing myself as a perpetual underdog, BMA seemed like a good match.

Out of a student body numbering roughly one hundred at the time, only five students were cross-country (a.k.a. nordic) skiers; the rest were downhill skiers (a.k.a. alpine). I enrolled at BMA in the fall of 1995 and moved into a host home provided by the Dalley family to save money on boarding costs. Not having Matt and Matt to identify with and rely on for support, I was forced into a situation where I didn't know anyone. My personality as a scared and lonely introvert was about to rear—what I then thought of as—its ugly head.

While I was riding in the car on the highway up to Burke for the first time, a terrifying anxiety swept over me. I vividly remember looking at a copy of BMA's newsletter, *News & Views*, during the drive, looking at pictures of all of these "cool kids" with envy, hoping that one day I would be as cool as they were. Crazy, because I didn't even know them; I was making up baseless assumptions in my head. Personally, I had not gained any self-confidence as a nordic skier yet; self-confidence, I understood, was a trait of being cool and likeable. Therefore, I had set myself up to be vulnerable the minute that I walked onto the beautiful and scenic campus that fall.

The illusion that I created about how to be "cool" and "uncool" would predominate my three-year tenure at BMA. My ego would help keep the narrative rolling in my head that I was "less than" and everyone else was "greater than." For the first time in my life, without Matt and Matt by my side to bolster my confidence, I was faced with making new friends on my own. It scared the living shit out of me.

At BMA, I was introduced to a new socioeconomic class driven by money. To my parents' credit, they leveraged themselves pretty heavily so that I could make this jump, taking out loans and asking for financial help from my grandparents. I am beginning to appreciate the financial strain that was put on our family so that I could afford the opportunity to attend an expensive ski academy. Because I was thrust into a new social stratum, I continued to perceive myself as an outcast, incapable of relating to my peers due to our differences. This was a natural misapprehension for a fifteen-year-old to have.

In order for a student to attend BMA, a family had to put up $20K to $25K per year, the equivalent of tuition at many colleges and universities. It wasn't cheap by any stretch of the imagination, especially mine. Walking around the campus during my first week at BMA, I saw other kids with expensive mountain bikes and nice clothes and who were speaking a special social language. It's hard to describe how irrelevant I felt within my new set of peers. Maybe their foreign accents (Australian, British, European, Russian, and Canadian) separated us. I was especially intimidated by the Australian students. To this day, I still don't know why. The girls looked older and more attractive; the guys had more hair on their bodies and were more developed, more mature. A sense of insecurity grew within me with the idea that this group of kids, tucked away in this boarding school in the northeast kingdom of Vermont, far away from families, was out to get me and prove me unworthy in relation to them. My true side of being an introvert started to bubble up, much in the same way that a paranoid schizophrenic doesn't want to leave the house for fear he or she will be attacked by strangers. Within a week, because I felt that I couldn't fit in at my new school, I almost called my parents to pick me up and bring me back home. I hated being at BMA.

During my first year, though, I ended up surviving, somehow pushing through the insecurities of being an outcast mostly because of the company of my fellow nordic skiers. There were only five of us: Forrest, Jordan, Erin, Jen, and me. Our coach, Jen Douglas (Dougie), completed the group. It was with these five people that I felt the most comfortable. Because they were fellow nordic skiers, I could relate to them on a level that I was incapable of with the rest of the BMA students. Other than with a couple of the other day students at BMA, I didn't make any close friends that year. I was so intimidated by everyone else that paralysis set in when I made an effort to talk to anyone. I may have tried, but I don't remember it.

One day, toward the end of my junior year, my teammate Jordan decided that it was time for me to break out of my shell. She recognized that I was lonely, so she forced me to walk around one of the dorms to hang out and get to know some of our classmates. It was a fucking frightening experience. The first dorm room we walked into was that of this gal Jenni. Luckily, her roommate, Mariah, someone I was intimidated by, wasn't there, so the three of us struck up a conversation. I was so nervous being there, mostly because I felt like I had nothing to contribute to the conversation. I probably didn't say a word. And if I did, I'm sure it didn't make any sense.

While I appreciated the effort that Jordan made in getting me out there among my peers, it certainly did not become a habit that she may have wanted to instill in me. I spent most days, in between classes and training, sitting alone in the day-student room, thinking about how much fun I was missing. In my mind, it was clear that everyone else at BMA was having so much more fun than I was. I began to loathe the fear of missing out—to the point where resentments started to boil.

In the spring of my junior year at BMA, the school had a bit of a melt-down regarding the "extracurricular" activities that were going on around campus after hours. Apparently, once the staff members left for the evening after dinner, BMA became one big party, flowing with copious amounts of alcohol, drugs, and sex. Word had it that one of the rich-kid students, Jimmy, would actually receive a package every Wednesday that was filled with all sorts of party favors. That year, still living with my host family, I rarely experienced BMA after hours. But it was at BMA that I first heard of the drugs called *ecstasy* and *cocaine*. Sheltered in the safe confines of Worthington, I was never exposed to these potential drug hazards. It was at this point in my life that I told myself that I was missing out, and if I were to ever be seen as cool by my peers, I would need to be involved in all of the shenanigans with the rest of the students. These intentions would shape my social career in college and later in life.

The northeast kingdom of Vermont is simply beautiful. Vermont is divided into three distinct sections: Burlington, the northeast kingdom, and every-thing else. For some reason, there was an aura and mystique that the king-dom encapsulated. Seemingly in the middle of nowhere, the largest town in the area was St. Johnsbury, followed closely in population by Lyndonville.

From a nonresident's point of view, the kingdom is stuck in the 1980s. When driving through Lyndonville for the first time, I remember seeing a dilapidated laundry repair shop, a replica of a can of Bag Balm hanging off the southern end of some commercial building, and, of course, the Lyndonville Diner. Modernization seemed to have skipped this part of Vermont, and I absolutely loved parts of it for some reason. It felt comfortable, as if I were still a kid going on weekend trips with my mom to Pittsfield to get bagels and hit the Stop 'N Shop for a week's worth of groceries.

Heading north out of Lyndonville on Route 114 toward the town of East Burke, one sensed that this old-fashioned era continued on forever, or at least to the border (Canada was about sixty miles to the north). The northeast kingdom mostly embodied a typical New England landscape, replete with small streams, rivers, forests, crumbling paved roads, and a mixture of pine and maple trees. Come fall, when the leaves changed, the scenery was picture perfect and exquisite. There were several towns in the area, such as Stannard, East Haven, and Victory, that barely registered as towns because of their low populations. One of my good friends, Forrest, lived in Stannard, which had a population of twenty-six! The main road, other than I-5 that headed north to Canada, was Route 114. Off 114 were multiple semipaved and dirt roads that seemed to have no name or destination except for, of course, Mountain Road, which led to BMA and to the ski resort atop Burke Mountain.

Some mysterious aura lingered in the northeast kingdom as a whole, even to a kid who grew up in a small, wooded town with a population of twelve hundred. For instance, to the north of Burke Mountain, as one combed the skyline for a glimpse into the never-ending forests of Vermont, one could discern an unexpected cluster of buildings, seemingly built with no purpose, on East Mountain. It was the strangest sight. A cold war relic, the old base was built to be a radar station for northern New England and to keep an eye out for enemy fire during World War II. Legend has it that the base never opened. What remained was a ghost town of barracks and radar towers. Being obsessed with the phenomena of UFOs and all things wacky, I was—and still am—convinced that the base was grand central for all sorts of weird occurrences. I only had the chance to visit the base once when Jordan, Erin, and I drove through the woods to go check it out one night. The three of us promptly turned around, scared shitless, when we thought we saw a ghost walking through one of the buildings.

Burke Mountain Resort was a hidden treasure. I was only accustomed to the western Massachusetts ski areas of Brodie, Bosquet, and Jiminy Peak: lots of crowds, not much vertical drop, and humble lodges. Burke Mountain Resort was different, with far more vertical and tougher terrain, much like some of New England's more prestigious resorts, such as Killington, Stratton, Sunday River, and Stowe.

Being a nordic skier, I really didn't understand the culture of alpine skiing entirely. I suppose I got a taste during my years at BMA. The time I spent on the mountain was not during winter but in the fall and spring when our team would hold dry-land training sessions on the mountain's trails. The views from the top of Burke Mountain were spectacular, especially because of the Willoughby Gap, which held a lake between two peaks, Willoughby Mountain and Mount Pisgah. The story goes that Lake Willoughby had underground tunnels to nearby lakes, alluding to the mystery of the northeast kingdom. I'm always up for believing a good conspiracy theory.

To the north of BMA lay East Mountain, the home of the unexplained military base. To the southeast lay perhaps the most impressive view of the picturesque New Hampshire peak, Mount Washington, tucked among the prominent White Mountains. At the time, having never seen the immense mountain ranges on the West Coast, I was awestruck by the grandeur of the surrounding hills. Mount Greylock, Massachusetts's tallest mountain, was pretty big, but it did not compare to my new surroundings in northern New England.

BMA was unusual among New England prep schools. The only real requirement for entry was that you had to be a ski racer in either the alpine or nordic disciplines. It was officially known as a ski academy, comparable to Stratton Mountain School (Matt and Matt's high school), Green Mountain Valley School, Carrabassett Valley Academy, and Killington Mountain School, among many others.

At BMA, success in academics was not measured by the typical letter grades (A, B, C, D, and F). The students followed a typical class schedule in normal high school subjects (e.g., math, English, science, foreign languages, and art). At the end of each term, rather than receiving grades, we were given written evaluations, which were taken very seriously by the academic and administrative staff. In fact, for me, a positive written evaluation meant so much more than a simple letter grade because they gave me a better sense of achievement. After an adjustment period from the traditional grading system, I began to thrive in the evaluation system, but it confused me when we began applying to colleges during my senior year.

One staff member, Tommy D., was the one who helped us put together our college entry applications without utilizing grade transcripts. The evaluation system seemed to work, as evidenced by students being regularly accepted to top-ranked schools, such as Middlebury, Williams, Dartmouth, St. Lawrence, Colby, and Bates.

While the education at BMA was important, most of the students were mainly there to train as elite high school athletes. Our daily routines were oriented around working out and exercise. A typical fall day (the time for prime dry-land training prep for the winter ski season) at BMA would go as follows: wake up; morning run/strength work; breakfast; classes till noon; lunch; dry-land training session; soccer practice (soccer was a required sport for all students); cross-country running practice; dinner; homework; and then sleep, only to wake up the next morning to start the process all over again. With all of the training that I do on my own now, I am truly beginning to appreciate the hard work and focus to which we dedicated ourselves when we were students. We had it pretty damn good back then.

My junior year continued to be a torturous emotional rollercoaster, even after a few months of integration into my new surroundings. Socially, I continued to be shy and awkward, always thinking that my classmates were relentlessly making fun of me. Living off-campus with the Dalleys didn't necessarily lend itself to my becoming a part of the BMA family. Yes, I was enrolled there, but the student body really bonded during evenings when I had gone home for the day. I was missing out on a key component of what it meant to be a BMA student. Furthermore, I created the narrative that because I was a day student, living off-campus, and a nordic skier, everyone thought I was a loser dipshit and dork. I tormented myself mentally, day in and day out, only finding solace when I spent time around my fellow day-student nordic skiers. I describe us as outcasts because, as I mentioned before, only 5 percent of the student body were nordic skiers. Everyone else was an alpine skier, which meant they had much more time to bond as teenagers while training. Plus, most of them couldn't grasp the concept of "running on skis," as my buddy Craig would say, when they were too busy flying down the mountain at insane speeds. I found that the two disciplines of ski racing fostered differences in the demeanors of those who participated in them.

In the spring of 1996, after the school year was over, I was relieved to return home to Worthington, my comfort zone, to regroup, finish going through puberty, and reflect on some of the misperceptions that I had conjured up in my own mind during my junior year. That year was absolutely exhausting. I didn't know how I was going to make it through another year at BMA.

My cross country ski teammates at Burke Mountain Academy from left to right: Erin, Jen (coach), Forrest, myself, Jordan, and Jen, 1996

Luckily, I did rustle up the nerve to return to the school the following fall. As a senior, I felt a little more at ease with being one of the elder students on campus, but my lack of confidence continued to shadow me. I slowly began to creep out of my shell. I managed to engage in conversation with all my classmates. I think I may have even had a girlfriend or two that year, which was a departure from my then normal behavior.

The fear of missing out still annoyed me. Based on what had happened during my junior year, I knew that BMA continued to be one big party that I wasn't attending. We, as nordic skiers, could throw on our skis and train right outside of our day-student room, which lay adjacent to the soccer fields. As I skied across the field, I fabricated this idea that every other student at school would be watching me ski from the dining hall, bullying me about what a loner I was and so unworthy of rating as "cool" kid. This narrative pounded my head for those first two years at BMA; I did not have the wherewithal to think otherwise. My mind was always telling me that I did not fit in, I wasn't cool enough, I wasn't rich enough, I wasn't fast enough, and I wasn't worthy of being included in the social cliques that formed at BMA. I began to feel helpless, confused, and paranoid; I projected that I would always be alone. This vision helped cement how I thought of myself during my late teenage years.

I wasn't terribly competitive at skiing my senior year, which made me feel severely self-conscious about my appearance and social status. I remember feeling out of place at ski races, even if Matt and Matt were there with their respective teams. The notion of positive self-worth had completely abandoned me. I used to have it within the ski community, especially before I got to BMA, because I was one of the top racers for my age during that time. Having a small amount of success as a skier helped me to define who I was. At BMA, my mind's voice did not stop saying, "You suck at skiing, Spence. You're weak, you're no good, you're a loser, and you're unattractive to boot." The negative energy compounded upon itself while the cycle got longer and heavier. By the time I had hit graduation in June of 1997, I had gone through the gambit of negative thinking and was pretty sure that I was going to be alone forever.

Deep inside, I wanted my experience at BMA to mean something. A week before graduation, I started developing another narrative that I remember telling Jordan. I stated to her, "I think a lot of feelings, truth, and emotions are going to come out from our class at graduation." In other words, toward *me*. My classmates would give me accolades as each stood up to talk briefly about his or her experience at the school. Then, the idea that I was "unlikeable" would be quashed. But when those accolades didn't come and graduation had passed, I was enormously disappointed in myself. Were the perceptions that I had created for myself, in fact, true?

Self-deprecating thoughts pervaded my Burke existence. I am still trying to figure out what that all meant. Even being twenty years removed from the situation, I have a recurring nightmare that I am back at BMA, intimidated beyond belief. In the dream, the experience of being the boy who felt so much insecurity about being around all of those "cool" kids comes back. When I wake up, I am completely relieved.

My talent as a potential division-one nordic skier had not yet developed by senior year, as I had hoped. I had not yet been recruited by any college to join its team. I had not achieved any significant results on the New England nordic ski circuit, so I didn't get noticed by the majority of college coaches. My applications to Middlebury, Colby, and Bates had all been denied or wait-listed. As the application rejections piled up and it became clear that I might need another year of development, I started to consider the unthinkable (at the time) of returning to Burke the next fall as a postgrad student. It made sense. Being younger than most of my nordic skiing counterparts, having another year as an "OJ" (older junior), I would have the extra year of training that might put me in better shape to be accepted in a division-one college. So I aimed for BMA in the fall of 1997.

I was hoping that going back to BMA as an "elder statesmen," and with all of my classmates having moved on to college, I could jumpstart my confidence and, at long last, enjoy my time without the stress of the years before. That notion, however, began to disintegrate quickly. As the summer of 1997 progressed, I gradually found out that there were others in my class who had the same idea as I did—to return for a postgrad year. I was truly looking forward to the chance to finally break out socially among my peers, to be the oldest at school, and to be away from the classmates I had graduated with the preceding June. The story that I had been telling myself, that no one in my class liked me, at last might subside. This was not the case. As the 1997–1998 school year approached, it became clear that I would have to confront the trepidations of being a social outcast yet again. It was ultimately arranged that the five postgrads would be living together in a condo up the hill from the main campus. I dreaded that not only would I have to return as a postgrad with a handful of kids who terrified me, but I would also be living with them.

That fall, because our condo was not very closely monitored, I discovered a way to relate to the rest of guys: booze. Tyler, one of my condo-mates, broke into the owner's closet to reveal a stash of liquor. Drinking didn't become a nightly ritual that year, but it became the crutch that I was looking for to help me get out of my head and supposedly feel comfortable.

My social "coming-out" party among many of my former classmates occurred on alumni weekend that fall, when most of them returned to visit the school. That weekend was the first time that I can recall using alcohol to fit into the BMA family. While being intoxicated that weekend, I realized that my former classmates actually liked me! I felt worthy; I felt like I fit in. The feeling was infectious, and I wanted more of it. I had spent the previous two years petrified and socially inept, and now I had a way to relieve the fear: to drink. Problem solved!

In the winter of 1998, I was still firmly focused on becoming a faster skier. After three years of consistent training under the BMA nordic program, I produced the results I had been seeking. Staying an extra year was beginning to pay dividends. Throughout that season, I rose through the junior New England ranks to be named to the Junior Olympic (JOs) team that traveled out west to Idaho to compete among the best junior ski racers in the country. Because of that experience, I started to be noticed by division-one college nordic ski coaches across New England. Now that I was in the "fast junior skiers" conversation in New England, the exposure to the top-tier ski schools became more and more prevalent. It felt really good and satisfying, strictly due to the reassurance that I was getting—that I was, in fact, a fast skier. The schools that had not even noticed me the year before were now taking an interest in my talents. Needless to say, it was flattering, and I soaked up the attention as best as I could. After going through my postgraduate year, I landed an offer to enroll at St. Lawrence University the following year and to contribute to their team's efforts to become a strong force on the New England college ski circuit.

Back at Burke, my social ineptitude eased. I started making friends with some of the younger students and became less anxious in group settings. I even started to let go around my condo roommates, from whom I had felt so much pressure during the previous two years. Life at Burke was finally becoming fun. I'm pretty certain that if it had not been for the drunken alumni-weekend experience that previous fall, I would not have reached the point where I could finally relate to my peers.

My self-reliance with females was improving as well. I had more female friends and girlfriends that year as a result of this enlivened confidence. Because I had falsely put alpine skiers on a pedestal during the previous two years, I never would have even approached a girl who competed as a down-hill skier just to talk, much less have a relationship with. Something had certainly changed in me. Perhaps being older helped; perhaps puberty had finally finished its bout with me. Whatever it was, having self-assurance that year around females became less and less of an issue. Had I finally joined the "cool kid" crowd?

Just as my life's momentum was picking up steam, socially, academically, and athletically, it almost came to a screeching halt. Since our post-grad condo remained mostly unmonitored by the BMA staff, we tended to have more extracurricular fun than was generally accepted on the BMA campus. We invited younger students who lived on campus to sneak out of their dorms and come up to the condo on a regular basis. Being the older kids, we thought we had it made because we could access alcohol; one of my roommates had a fake ID. For high school kids, of course, we were the guys to admire.

My roommates and I became careless about hiding all of the fun we were having at the condo. For us postgrads, living off campus was a potential recipe for disaster. The administrative staff and headmaster caught wind of what was happening. It was only a matter of time before we got nailed for something specific. That day came, much to our dismay, and it came at right about the time that I was feeling on top of the world.

At BMA, an honor code is strictly enforced by the staff. Within the code, transgressions that will not be tolerated are listed. I'm guessing the staff knew that some of the individual students were not saints. But, in a group, if those students created a situation that started to boil over, the headmaster would call a school meeting in the dining hall to address the matters at hand. That meeting was a chance for the students to admit to what they had done, to clear the air and come clean. Based on past experience, the staff had found that this method of communal coming-clean was an effective way to address troubling circumstances. And so, in the winter of 1998, Finn, our headmaster, called for a meeting.

As students filed into the dining hall, it became apparent that my condo roommates and I were the center of the investigation. Whispers were going around the student body, prior to the meeting, that the five of us were being targeted for our bad behavior, knowledge of which eventually filtered down to the underclassmen. After four hours in which many students admitted to wrongdoing, it became clear that we postgrads were likely going to be expelled from BMA. If the staff's plan played out, it would spell certain doom for my college acceptance. Even though I had earned my high school diploma, St. Lawrence would not have looked kindly on my expulsion as a postgraduate student.

For the next week, with my college and skiing career in jeopardy, my mom got on the phone to lobby for BMA to keep me on. I learned she made incessant phone calls to both Finn and my coach, James. During this process, the confidence I had amassed was quickly crashing down. I had fucked up, and I was going to pay the consequence. My social coming-out party that year was beginning to backfire. I figured it was my fate to always be an introvert, incapable of fitting in among my peers. That week of waiting on the administration's decision was pure torture; everything was at stake.

My mom's persistence on the phone paid off. Finn decided to keep me enrolled as a postgrad until the end of the winter race season. In order to stay on, my roommates and I had to meet certain conditions. Apart from meals and training, we were allowed no access to the rest of the student body, which, for me, wasn't a big deal, once I understood the benefit of having the next four years of my life unaffected. St. Lawrence would never have to know what happened that winter, and my acceptance and future enrollment wouldn't be called into question because of my misbehavior. In fact, going through that experience at such a critical time in my life gave me a good perspective on the degree to which my actions could affect my future.

Unfortunately, once I arrived at St. Lawrence, those lessons were all for naught. The struggles that I experienced at BMA as an insecure and seemingly helpless teenager shaped me into the person that I am today, but it wasn't necessarily all for the best.

In a twist of irony, Matt Whitcomb, who went to Stratton Mountain School, would eventually become the head nordic ski coach at BMA. Later on, he would go on to buy land and build his own cabin in East Burke. It took me several years, from a psychological standpoint, to finally visit his small plot of land. I had not been to BMA in fourteen years; I was scared and ashamed to visit. The moment I stepped back onto the BMA campus, a flood of emotions ranging from pleasant to terrifying came over me. I remember sneaking gulps of whiskey from a bottle that I hid in my jacket during that trip to numb me out a bit. I couldn't surmount my embarrassment otherwise.

After visiting, though, I saw the town of Burke and BMA in a new light. Afterward, all I could think about was what it would be like to move to the northeast kingdom and build the area and community into an East Coast trail-running ultra-mecca of sorts. I still think about that possibility.

I left BMA in 1998, nineteen years ago. Since being sober, I understand, apart from my insecurities, that those years turned me into a forward thinker. I am grateful that my parents made financial sacrifices to allow me to leave home at age fifteen while unintentionally exposing me to the hardships and vulnerabilities of adolescence in an environment that was not home. My memories, discounting the uneasy dreams that wake me up in the middle of the night, of Burke Mountain Academy are fond.

CHAPTER 8

Summer 2012

The year I plunged headfirst into running ultra-marathons was 2012. An ultra-marathon is technically any race longer than the 26.2-mile distance of a marathon. My first ultra-distance race, the McDonald Forest 50K (31.1 miles), was the most humbling experience of my athletic career to date. I got my ass kicked. My finishing time was around six hours and fifteen minutes; when I'm in shape, I have the capability to run that race in 4:20 hours to 4:30 hours. Two weeks prior, I had run a 3:03:00 at the Eugene Marathon, a personal record (PR) for me as well as a respectable qualifying time for the Boston Marathon. Therefore, it wasn't necessarily a wonder that I got throttled running up and down the endless hills in Corvallis's own McDonald-Dunn Forest. I wasn't nearly recovered enough from the marathon. That's what I told myself.

After consulting with Mike, my coach at the time, I figured it would be a good time to jump into the 50K distance without delay, anticipating that the majority of the summer was going to be dedicated to the process of preparing for the 2012 TransRockies Run, a six-day, 120-mile stage race in the heart of the Colorado Rockies. Brian, my friend who had pulled my drunk ass out of bed to go running with him back in 2007, proposed the idea to run TransRockies as a team. Without hesitation, I said yes. With that, I signed up and raced the McDonald Forest 50K. The obscure sport of running unthinkable and insanely long distances in the woods was going to be mine.

As the summer of 2012 progressed, with TransRockies looming a couple of weeks ahead, I thought it might be a good idea to test the waters and run another 50K event to pump up my confidence. I signed up for the Siskiyou Out & Back (SOB) 50K, which is held annually in July in Ashland, Oregon, one the nation's premier trail-running locations. Ashland remains a town where some of the fastest ultra-runners in the country reside. Luckily, my fitness had progressed so much since the Mac 50K that I was able to take nearly an hour off of my time in a couple of months. The accomplishment, in and of itself, was a turning point in the development of my certainty that I could tackle distances and terrains that the TransRockies Run promised. In fact, I was so proud of my accomplishments at the SOB 50K that after the race I went straight to a bar in Ashland and got fucking hammered beyond belief, all by myself.

At that time, I wasn't necessarily convinced that I had an issue with alcohol. I still felt like I could control my cravings. However, I used the accomplishment of the SOB 50K as an excuse to drink myself into oblivion. Hell, I "deserved a reward for my success," a mantra-to-be for the future. This type of behavior repeated itself over and over. I chose to ignore the irritant of denial that lay deep within my soul. Excuses to drink came in the form of big life events, whether positive or negative. I would regress into consuming alcohol to handle the emotions and anxiety that arose for unknown reasons. Getting drunk was a way to quell the constant confusion that my mind would present to me. You know, to avoid those persistent narratives that tended to swirl around in my head.

Minutes after the SOB 50K had finished, I went to an Irish pub in downtown Ashland to watch the day's rerun of the Tour de France. Alone, I put down more than a dozen beers and several shots of Crown Royal Whiskey. Why couldn't this bad-ass athlete reward himself with excessive amounts of alcohol? Sure, it was OK to both drink and be an athlete with no consequences. No one really had to know what I was doing; it was my little secret. Combining these apparent skills boosted my self-image, identity, and confidence to the nth degree.

After getting shit-faced, I decided to call it a day and wandered back to my hotel room, plastered, to bask in the day's accomplishments with one more nightcap of Crown Royal.

Having ultimately blacked out the night before, I woke up in my hotel room feeling guilty and with a heavy-duty hangover. Stopping for breakfast on my way back home to Corvallis, I paired my guilt with my growing loneliness and depression and decided that maybe I should try to stop drinking. Maybe the booze wasn't so good for my athletic endeavors. That was my excuse. And I could stand to lose a couple of pounds in preparation for TransRockies. Monday, July 16, 2012, was the date that I first attempted sobriety.

To stop drinking at that point wasn't much of a challenge. I just kind of stopped drinking. No detailed explanation was necessary other than I felt better overall because I had eliminated hangovers and had more energy day to day, especially to run. As July rolled into August, I met Brian in Colorado to try our shot at racing the TransRockies Run. The race and experience was incredibly influential and downright inspirational. Running the TransRockies, as well as the SOB 50K and Mac 50K, triggered an infatuation with the community and spirit that seemed to dominate the sport of ultra-running. Even though I was forced to drop out of the TransRockies due to an injury, I returned home to Corvallis fired up to take my newfound sport more seriously. I wasn't drinking, so maybe I could really get good at running for the first time in my life.

Corvallis was the perfect spot to try to figure out how to run ultramarathons; it has an unbelievable trail system coupled with an enthusiastic, under-the-radar trail-running community. My playground was set; all I needed was to continue to embrace the enthusiasm for the sport that I had developed throughout the summer. As summer turned to fall, the enthusiasm and passion could only grow.

For the following months, sobriety was a breeze. Drinking never crossed my mind, even at social events. Even though college football season was in gear, habitually a prime time for me to get fucked up, I stayed dry. The gains made in my endurance and my capacity to run long distances encouraged me. Training runs of more than twenty miles in the mountains became routine. Losing weight served as another boost to my self-confidence. I was largely on cruise control until Lisa reached out to me in early November.

Fucking Lisa, she always had a tendency to throw me off track. And, once again, she succeeded. I had gotten my hands on a couple of tickets to the Civil War (the Oregon State Beavers versus University of Oregon Ducks football game), and since I hadn't seen her in quite a while, I invited her to join me at the game. She was a diehard Ducks fan, so I figured she would appreciate the gesture. Because of our history with partying, our predilection for drinking and drugging when she came to Corvallis for the game might prove irresistible. Once the anticipation took an undeniable hold on me, I made up my mind that during Civil War, I would allow myself a cheat day and drink. Just one day, that was all. Maybe Lisa would finally admit to me that I was the one for her. With her unpredictable nature, hope was never lost.

On my way to pick up Lisa, I calmly and intentionally stopped at a convenient corner store just outside of Corvallis and bought a few roadies to celebrate my cheat day. The roadies were for Lisa, too, to have on the car ride back to the game. I was trying to be a gentleman. By the time Lisa was in my car, the inevitable party began. On the way back to Corvallis for the game, we dove into snorting a bunch of chopped-up Adderall (basically amphetamines for treating ADHD) and pounding beers.

As the day progressed, things got out of hand. Right around the fourth quarter of the game, I slipped into a full-on blackout. Lisa and I spent what must have been only ten minutes in the stands watching the game. The winner was a mystery to me. In fact, as long as she was with me and we were getting hammered together, why bother to watch the game, right? Seemed like the right choice to me. We spent the majority of the afternoon tailgating with strangers who offered us a variety of exotic drinks. We partied our asses off.

Hours later, after the game had ended, I woke up in my bed, unaware of how I had gotten home from the game. My car was in the parking lot, so that was a good sign. Lisa was still with me, and she woke up at the same time I did. After wiping our sleep-ridden eyes and deciding that this night shouldn't end so early, we chopped up more of her Adderall on my kitchen counter, snorted it, and reset ourselves. Following a few glasses of champagne, we decided that it would be a fantastic idea to drive to Eugene to keep on rolling. She had family down there, so we had a place to stay. With that in mind, fully buzzed up, we got in my car and made the forty-mile drive down south on the back roads along Highway 99W. When I was drunk, driving was never a problem. On a road that is normally heavily patrolled by cops, if I had been pulled over that night, I would have been arrested on the spot and thrown in jail—a done deal. Clouded by the thrill of having Lisa, Adderall, and road sodas in my car simultaneously, I didn't give a fuck. Miraculously, our adventure that night didn't end up with a crashed car, a DUI, or even a death of some innocent being, much less our own deaths. Once in Eugene, Lisa and I toasted ourselves for being good drunk drivers. Within twenty minutes of safely parking the car, we rolled into a dive bar and stayed until the wee hours of the next morning.

When winter hit that year, my dedication to becoming sober dissipated. My brief stint of being dry was a distant memory. The next few months after that football game, I went on a self-induced bender of epic proportions. Lisa had lit another fire in me to pursue her in any way possible. The seal of sobriety was broken in November. With the upcoming holidays around the corner, when everyone drinks, I chose to mindlessly remain unsober, totally ignoring any promise to myself to quit. My indulgence in excess lasted for another year and half.

CHAPTER 9

St. Lawrence University sits at the top of upstate New York. Not like New Paltz, Kingston, or Albany upstate. It's like Canada upstate. It's a tundra landscape of cows, hayfields, seedy dive bars, and small remote towns, two hours north of the Adirondack Mountains in Canton, New York, truly in the middle of nowhere, just about ninety minutes or so south of Canada's capital, Ottawa. That geographic fact was convenient because the drinking age was eighteen in Canada, which was my age freshmen year. The town of Canton actually *is* St. Lawrence University (SLU), the only game in town in terms of industry and, possibly, employment.

SLU and BMA had similar reputations and characteristics. From my perspective, SLU kids, like most students at BMA, came from money. Perhaps I was hyper-biased to think so. But in the late 1990s and early 2000s, the years of my attendance, SLU seemed to be the safety school for the rich kids who came from DC, New York City, and Boston. I could've sworn that my freshman dorm was 90 percent full of kids from Greenwich, Connecticut, one of the richest towns in the country. Furthermore, the school seemed to be fully populated with students who would have preferred to attend Ivy League schools—like Brown, Dartmouth, and Harvard—had their grades in high school met the acceptable standard.

The campus was peppered with Land Cruisers, Beamers, and the mandatory sprinkling of Audis. It was my impression that most students had their cars purchased for them by either their parents or by means of fancy trust fund accounts. I had fellow students and friends, aptly named "trustafarians," who would walk around campus in their Carhartts and flannels, trying to blend in with the country folk, being cool as fuck, knowing that even if they screwed up at school, they'd have an eight-figure trust fund waiting in the wings to catch them. I was downright jealous of them: I didn't come from money.

St. Lawrence was, regrettably, an institution where one's actions produced very few consequences, where a student could do whatever the hell he or she wanted, sometimes having total disregard for a conduct policy or the law itself. Having spent an extra year at BMA to hone my skills as a skier, I walked onto campus in the fall of 1998 as an older freshman. Having a step up on most of my classmates and peers, my confidence glowed. The money thing still intimidated the hell out of me, but far less than it did at BMA.

From the outset, my hopes for thriving at SLU were high. Repeating the emotionally scarring experience that I had gone through at BMA was not an option. The thoughts of being an introvert at my new school scared the hell out of me. I was prepared to do anything in my power to avoid feeling lonely and like I was on the outside looking in. Enter alcohol, endless amounts of alcohol.

The first weekend at SLU was fucking profound, awesome, and insane. During orientation I had met a couple of good dudes and even a few girls. Being the fastest freshmen skier on the cross-country ski team sustained my self-esteem. Throw in some fine Canadian Labatt's Blue Lager, and I was flying high. There I was: being social, likeable, boisterous, fun, outspoken, and fucking cool, a far cry from recoiling from the social scene, which had happened during the previous years at BMA.

The first party I attended on campus opened me up to another world. People approached me, asked my name, and seemed interested in who I was. Even this slamming-hot blond girl came up to me to tell me I was hot! Unfortunately, not ten minutes later, she left with the captain of the hockey team. Having made a 180-degree personality turn, within two weeks I acquired more friends at SLU than I did during my entire three years spent at BMA. The seeming reality of suddenly opening up convinced me that it was going to be easy to flourish at college. All I had to do to keep the momentum going was to hold on to booze, my new secret weapon, and keep it at the forefront of my life. The term "liquid courage" came to seriously define itself.

No one else could have had a better freshman year at college than I did. Almost immediately I met Hillary, a fellow skier, albeit downhill, who turned out to be my girlfriend for the better part of the next year and a half. In addition, my entourage of friends grew quickly to include Jeff, Courtney, Brian, Kieran, Harvey, Marchetti, Zach, Wadowski, Brent, Pepper, among many others. A core group of friends would only evolve over the next four years. At BMA, my group of friends amounted to just a few, and that group took three years to build. College offered an easy atmosphere to bond with new friends in a short amount of time. I very quickly became accustomed to the comfort and reliability of friendship.

Even Matt and Matt came to visit from their college, Middlebury, because the socializing and partying was so great and out of control at SLU. I was overly anxious and proud to introduce them to my new extended family. The sons of senators and heirs to big businesses, like Tower Records, were my buddies. That sort of high-end association at BMA was rare; my links with that crowd at SLU were numerous. Within my freshman year, I forged relationships with people from all walks of life: the Outing Club, the Greek system, the rich jocks, the nerds, and basically students from every faction thinkable. Every single thing about it was great.

My practice of drinking never waned. This train was never going to stop. With a positive change of attitude and escalation in self-assurance, I continued to forge ahead and capitalize on my college experience. My sophomore year, Jeff, Kieran, Brian, Gallo, and I pledged a fraternity, Phi Kappa Sigma, one of the five such Greek houses at SLU. This move solidified my ego-filled, drunk, and riotous time at SLU. By joining, more than thirty new supposed friends entered my life. I didn't have to search for these guys to party with all the time. SLU was becoming my kingdom!

By sophomore year, I basically knew everyone around campus. I was acquiring the best image ever as likeable, caring, fun-loving, cool, athletic, adventurous, and fun as hell to party with. My sheltered BMA character was expressing itself differently at SLU. My primary goal when I moved onto the SLU campus was to never again be the dorky, nerdy, quiet introvert that I grew up as. It was such a relief knowing that I had successfully made the shift. I couldn't get enough of my new lifestyle.

During spring break of sophomore year, my friend Jeremy and I were on our way to meet up with a group of friends in the Outer Banks, North Carolina. Upon our arrival at the house where we were staying, my phone rang. It was my mom; she was frantic. All she said was that she and Dad were sitting in the kitchen and that Dad had just told her that he wanted a divorce. "What the fuck? Is this a sick joke?" Within hours of arriving in North Carolina, I got back into the car and drove all the way back home to Massachusetts.

As I walked into the house, the tension between my mom and dad was unbearable. It was true: he was leaving the family. Indelible in my memory is seeing the stoicism in my dad's face as he caught on to the fury stirring in my mom and me. After about an hour of poignant, yet angry, discussion between my dad and me, my dad left the house. Never could I have imagined that my parents would get a divorce. To witness the act of his leaving made no sense; I was severely resentful and pissed off. So I responded accordingly and drank as hard as I could for the next two months and into the summer, nonstop and out of fucking control. Drinking was the only means to numb the pain.

Heading into my junior year, my aspirations of being a competitive skier began to dwindle. The partying and socializing began to catch up with me. I was finally putting on the "freshman fifteen" they talk about—the obligatory weight gain that comes on when kids go off to college. Luckily, my first two years of skiing kept the weight off. But by missing workouts and staying up late with my rabble-rousing crew, it was inevitable that the pounds would accumulate. I had moved into the Phi Kap house, a place that didn't necessarily promote and support the idea of my being a competitive division-one skier. My housemates even sabotaged my efforts at being a competitive athlete. That fall, I literally faked my way onto the team; I had built up so many years of base endurance that I could get by pretty easily without doing much consistent training. The new coach, Jim (the "albino rhino," as we called him), started noticing my lack of fitness and empty attitude. It was pretty obvious that skiing was no longer a priority. I had become a professional at another sport: kicking ass at being a college kid.

My motivation for being an athlete wound down. Heading into the Christmas break that year, I made peace with the idea that it was time to call it quits with cross-country skiing. As our team van pulled up to the campus ski office, having participated in a training camp in Maine, I was ready to turn the page into a new chapter of life that excluded skiing.

While on the road a couple of hours beforehand, I alerted some of my Phi Kap boys that I was saying good-bye to my athletic aspirations and quitting the ski team. With overwhelming approval of my decision, they began to prepare for my return home. I said a few quick good-byes to my teammates. Ironically, Phi Kap was located just across the parking lot from the ski office. I crossed the parking lot and met up with my boys waiting on the porch of the house. With whiskey in hand, I dropped my skis and catapulted straight into phase two of my college experience: total fucking decadence.

I grabbed my boy Buffy's bottle of liquor, opened my mouth, and began to guzzle, yielding to a monster that would capture me for the next eighteen years of my life. Little did I know that on this evening, the road to full-blown alcoholism was being paved.

Having quit the ski team, I felt liberated from the years of the pressure that accompanied being a competitive athlete. It lifted the instant I walked away. At first, it was a significant event in life to celebrate. I no longer had the responsibility of showing up for long runs on Sunday mornings with the team, and 6:00 a.m. strength/gym sessions became a thing of the past. In a matter of a few days, I changed every habit in my life that I had maintained for the last several years. The old habits gave way to new ones, such as Monday's UBU-IPA (a local microbrew) nights at the Glass Onion, Tuesday's Labatt Blue night at the Hoot Owl, Wednesday's flip-cup night at the Tick Tock, Thursday night's party wherever the party was, and Friday and Saturday frat parties and mixers to the extreme. To cap it off, Sunday nights in the library pretending to study with friends took on a new form: blowing Adderall and drinking while reading books about the history of economics and Rocks for Jocks, also known as Geology 101. Mapping out which girls were sitting where in the library also became a ritual.

My junior year saw the obliteration of my life. My mind and body totally changed. The more substances I put into myself, the worse I felt. My body was starting to recognize that quitting the ski team profoundly altered it. In place of the natural endorphins that I was accustomed to receiving on a daily basis as an athlete, I was supplying myself with other types of endorphins, paying no attention to the long-term ramifications.

Until I graduated in 2002, darkness encroached on my life each day. My senior year at St. Lawrence was pitch black. It was during the first semester of senior year that a buddy of mine introduced me to a new sensation. There was no doubt that I had spent the past year indulging in excessive behavior. However, the ante was about to be raised. One evening in the fall of 2001, when our semester's pledges were inducted into the fraternity, Chris pulled me aside and asked if I wanted a bump. "Of Adderall?" Sure, I was always down for some Addies. "Nah," he responded. "I've got something better." Enter cocaine. The second that shit found its way into my system, I was in love. Excessive drinking was still fun, but it was losing its overall spark and glamour. I needed more. Once coke entered the picture, I successfully relit the fire and my enthusiasm for a good party. Believing that it was impossible to sustain my current destructive tendencies through graduation, I now had found the way out.

Rebooted with an ambition that I could succeed, I continued to abuse drugs that year. They served as partners in crime, and we thrived until the day I graduated. Interestingly enough, when I got more into speed, the relationships I had built around campus since freshman year started to wane. The fact that I knew everyone and that I was known around campus still held true. But the energy I had put into achieving that status was no longer as important to me as getting fucked up. I cannot remember even a two-day stretch when I was not hammered.

For much of my senior year, my best Nikki Sixx impression of his dark days in the mid-to late 1980s dominated. I even had the leather pants to prove it. One Saturday in the spring of 2002, during the final countdown to graduation day, I took this emulation of my '80s rock-star hero as far as I could without going to full-on junkie mode. It was just another typical day for me. Buffy and I had started the party early at the Phi Kap house by sipping mimosas (substituting the champagne with warm Natty Ice). Fortunately for us, one of the sororities, Kappa Kappa Gamma, was throwing its annual Kegs and Eggs party at the Tick Tock, potentially the dirtiest—as in absolutely filthy—bar in all of the north country of New York. After getting good and primed off of our brilliant poor-as-fuck senior concoction, we made our way down to the bar to turn up the action.

It was 11:00 a.m. as Buffy and I sat at the bar, pounding Coors Lights (at this point we were the only people there) and slowly renewing the high from the night before. The sensation hit me that I could possibly black out three times within a twenty-four-hour span. Sickly, that possibility got me excited; it was a different source of achievement. Having blacked out once already after a full-on rager at Phi Kap's off-campus house and dusted by the fleeting thought about continual blackouts, I snapped out of it and chugged another Coors Light. There's a certain romance that goes along with hammering shitty beers during the day; I could never explain its appeal. It just felt right, sexy, and deviant. After a few hours of getting fucked up with Buffy and the Kappa girls, I slipped into a second blackout. One more to go!

The next several hours are lost from my memory. Somehow that afternoon I wandered my way back toward campus. I wasn't sure where Buffy went, though. I wondered if he had passed out in a ditch somewhere, much like I had done during the previous weekend. On this particular occasion, I was so fucked up that Jamal, the captain of the SLU soccer team, pulled me off the sidewalk in the early afternoon after I passed out in broad daylight. It's probably fair to say that he saved my ass that day. Who's to say I wouldn't have suffocated lying facedown, passed out, in a pile of dirty, gravel-laced snow.

Later on, still in a complete blackout, a bunch of the boys and I found our way into one of the main dining halls on campus. A concert was being played there later that night. Luckily, after getting some food into my system to help counteract the drinking I had been doing since 7:00 a.m., I began to crawl out of my blackout. As always, food seemed to be a proper remedy for coming back to life from a blackout. The next thing I remember is being on stage with an electric guitar, microphones, and amps plugged in, belting out a despicable version of the Poison anthem, "Every Rose Has Its Thorn." It was fucking epic. I had an audience of about one hundred in front of me, holding lighters in the air, singing along to every note. Goddamn, I thought, I have become Nikki fucking Sixx.

The story goes that while I was eating to overcome my drunkenness, I decided that it was a good idea to serenade the entire dining hall. I had the stage, the lights, the guitar, and the look so that I could realize my yearlong dream: to be a motherfuckin' rock star. After my fifteen minutes of fame were up, I regrouped with the boys and made my way back to the Tick Tock for another Saturday evening of chaos. And yes, once again, I blacked out. With flying colors, I actualized the sensation that I had had earlier that morning. In the last twenty-four hours I had been to the Tick Tock *three* times, and I had blacked out *three* times. My justification for the self-destruction was that I, for once, seized the opportunity to be a rock star. I had successfully established my new standard for the perfect day.

⸻⸺⸻

Other than being a screw-off during the last year and a half at St. Lawrence, I was still able to be somewhat productive. First, I was elected president of Phi Kappa Sigma. That honor provided me with my own suite in the house for senior year. Honestly, I just wanted the title; I had no interest in actually running a fraternity. Having the privacy to party on my own terms was added to the bragging rights that I was the alpha (a.k.a. the president) of my fraternity. Furthermore, having my own space meant that I had the chance to appreciate the excitement of drinking by myself. Eventually, I successfully nailed down that craft.

Second, while knowing I was taking a nose dive mentally and emotionally, I began doing some work with a therapist. His name was Daniel. Every Monday morning throughout senior year I would sit with Daniel, while sporting a mean hangover, and tell him about all of the cool shit I had done since our last meeting. I'm glad he didn't report me to anyone in the administration. Thank god for confidentiality agreements. As Daniel and I built more trust, I became aware of being more forthcoming about more than college life. It was during our later sessions that Daniel and I spoke about the concept of depression. I was cognizant of the possibility that I could be depressed, given my mom's history with it. By talking about it with Daniel, I understood that depression might be something I'd have to face later in life. But not now—I was too busy fucking off with all of my friends. I was in no position to make a change with so little time left at my consequence-free home in the north country of New York.

Senior year at St. Lawrence University with my buddies Crick (center) and Jeff (right). After I quit skiing my junior year, partying became my new focus, 2002

As spring rolled into early summer at SLU, I began to see the light at the end of the tunnel, so to speak, in considering the onset of another lifestyle shift. After graduation day, I knew that I was going back to Bend, a place where righting the ship, after mentally and physically destroying myself since 2000, was possible. I remember distinctly one instance where I thought about returning as an athlete. I had been invited by some of my ex-cross-country ski teammates to play a game of ultimate Frisbee. Although reluctant, because of how it would impede my partying schedule, I joined them to run around the soccer field to dive after tiny discs flying through the air. After a few minutes of clowning around, perhaps due to a natural endorphin release, I considered getting back into shape once I got out of Canton, hopefully unscathed.

While this group and I were having a blast on the field, a sense of innocence hit me, something I had not felt since quitting the ski team. Some kind energy and life hit me that reminded me of the past. Briefly, the booze and the drugs lost their hold on me. The freedom from booze didn't last much longer than the two hours that morning. I began to get antsy about the parties I was missing back on campus. Within minutes of leaving the soccer field, I went straight back to my room, took several shots of shitty vodka, snorted a few lines of Adderall, and got the rest of my day going. It was 11:00 a.m., and the day was full of promise.

As finals in the spring semester became imminent, my substance abuse issue was reaching an all-time high. Being a reckless, washed-up senior, I failed to legitimately prepare for what would hopefully be the last week of tests in my lifetime. Rather than being concerned with qualifying for graduation, my mind was focused on Senior Week, the postfinals week-long drunk fest leading to commencement. Furthermore, there were a few girls who needed some attention.

The last few days leading up to finals, I was able to score a handful of study drugs that were more potent than my regular dose of Adderall. I had no idea what they were, and I didn't care. In a panic, I stayed up for two straight days, rotating between the twenty-four-hour library room and my room at Phi Kap, to shotgun the most basic concepts of my courses into my memory bank. To my surprise, all the shit I put into my body worked. Finals went great—as in I didn't fail. Until the very last one. On Friday morning, the last day of finals, at 8:30 a.m. in a room full of "rock" nerds, I was handed my copy of the final for Geology 101. The instant I looked down at the first set of questions, I had this vision of Matt, a dutiful geology major at Middlebury, snickering at me. I had spent years making fun of him for being a "rock" nerd; for once, I was envious of his knowledge. As I flipped through the final, I was at a loss for the answers to the questions. I knew I was fucked. If I didn't pass this final somehow, I would be doomed to another year of college. I had neglected to take an Adderall before the exam. Rookie move on my part. If I studied and took tests with that drug in my system, I would win.

This time, with my ass on the line, I had dropped the ball. After spending about thirty minutes debating what I was going to do to get out of this, I was struck with a fabulous idea. Fortunately, a friend of mine who was sitting next to me at the exam was smart as hell. I knew she would nail down a 4.0 without even blinking an eye. With time running out, as she was crushing the exam, I passed her a note that said, "I'm fucked." Understanding the relative urgency of the situation, she hesitantly moved closer to me so that I could start copying her answers. After fifteen minutes of doing this, I had completed the exam. With a distorted sense of accomplishment, I stood up, grabbed my exam, handed it to the professor, and calmly walked out of the classroom. I knew that I had passed. After four years and several tens of thousands of dollars spent on room, board, and classes, I had completed my collegiate career—scholastically, that is. I cheated in order to graduate from St. Lawrence University.

Now that the nuisance of final exams was over, the real party could begin. I remember walking back to Phi Kap with my hands in the air, ready to celebrate. An aura of invincibility pulsed through my blood stream. Hearing AC/DC's "Hells Bells" blaring from Jeff's room at the house, I could imagine the promise of absolute fucking chaos for the next seven days. By 10:00 a.m. that Friday morning, I had successfully put a fifth of whiskey into my system. Bring on Senior Week!

My recollection of the week leading up to commencement is vague. I went through one or two blackouts a day, every day, preparing for my exodus from Canton. Booze, drugs, Adderall, you name it, I took it. My favorite concoction that week was to take every prescription pill that I could find, chop it up into one pile, and snort it all. It was called the "party mix." Senior Week met all my expectations. The following Sunday, it was fortunate that I was sober enough to walk among the class of 2002 to receive my diploma from President Sullivan and St. Lawrence University. By walking across that stage, a massive page had just turned for me.

Rather than rush home to Worthington to begin packing for my upcoming trip to Bend, I holed up in my buddy Brian's apartment in Canton, on his couch, to begin detoxing from the last year and a half. I remember being consumed, headfirst, by his oversized couch. I was absolutely exhausted.

It took me two days of lying on Brian's couch to work up the motivation to begin the drive home. I had the shakes, torrential anxiety, and a cloud of shame over my head. I felt depressed, unworthy, fat, repulsive, dirty, and glum. I finally put myself together enough to attempt the five-hour drive back home to Massachusetts. With Brian's help, I managed to pack up the last of my shit. As I started my car that morning to do one last drive through the north country of New York, I rolled my window down and told Brian, "It's time to get back to my roots, man." The destruction, turmoil, and stress of living the life of a reckless college student was over. At my core, I was broken. It was time to set things straight. To do something good, something healthy, and to find something to look forward to in life. I knew, in my heart of hearts, that I couldn't sustain the party for much longer. It was time for a change.

CHAPTER 10

August 2007

Driving home from my fancy job of selling overpriced lots of dirt, I picked up some malt liquor from the Alfalfa Market for drinking on the way home. Then Lauren called. By this time, she had made her way to Baltimore to begin settling into our new town. At first, the conversation was not antagonistic. We chatted for twenty minutes or so about the day's events before the tone changed abruptly. I was almost home. I casually disposed of the beer cans out the passenger-side window while driving around the corner onto Brosterhous Road. And the yelling began.

Lauren was obsessing over one of my ex-girlfriends, Vanessa, of whom she was dangerously jealous. How jealous she was I really didn't know but would soon find out. Lauren had learned that I had seen Vanessa a couple of weeks prior at a BBQ hosted by some mutual friends. She had curiously withheld confronting me about the incident. But not now. Lauren was letting loose on the phone as I pulled into my driveway. The accusations began to fly out of her mouth: I was a bad fiancé who couldn't be trusted and a shameful human being. "Act like a man," she said. "How am I ever going to trust you?" I never had the balls to repel the accusations that Lauren hurled at me.

Walking through the door, I grabbed a full bottle of red wine, acknowledged Brian, who was sitting on the couch, and continued the yelling match as I made my way upstairs to my bedroom. Brian was spooked by what he had witnessed. I'm not sure if he had ever seen me so enraged.

During the screaming, I cracked open the bottle of wine and remained in shock over all of the accusations flying my way. I was so fucking pissed off. My blood was boiling. Before hanging up on me, Lauren threw out the notion that I was cheating on her with Vanessa. After the phone went dead, I slammed it to the floor. Injected with panic, anxiety, and anger, I sat on my floor and started to chug down one of Oregon's finest Pinot Noirs straight out of the bottle.

After five minutes of serious, though drunken, contemplation, I made my way to the bathroom to get a bottle of Percocet that I had conned out of my oral surgeon after I promised him that I'd make an appointment to extract my wisdom teeth (not surprisingly, the appointment was never made; I wanted the pills). Having a lethal amount of painkillers in one hand and wine in the other, I looked back and forth between my two hands, contemplating my next step. Before I had the chance to act, an excruciating wave of frustration hit me. While lying in my empty stairwell, which was adorned with some of my mom's best artwork, I punched the wall and screamed at the top of my lungs. Totally freaked out at this point, Brian came to my rescue. He found me on the midlevel of my stairwell, crying, kicking, screaming, and intent on ending my life with the mixture of wine and pills that I was gripping in my hands. With that, he picked me up and demanded that I get in his car. If Brian had not been at my house that night, I would have ended my life. Brian had just saved it.

Brian had been through this type of situation before with another friend. Having the hindsight and gumption to decide that I needed professional help, he drove me straight to the emergency room at Bend's St. Charles Hospital. After admitting me, Brian left for home to process what he had gone through with one of his best friends. In a state of disbelief, I lay in my hospital bed, not really understanding what I had come close to attempting. Fucking suicide. Later that night, after my vitals had balanced out, I checked in to Sageview Psychiatric Center across the street from the hospital. I was still drunk.

CHAPTER 11

n June of 2002, at the conclusion of an epic bender at St. Lawrence, I decided to head back to Bend, Oregon. The town had become my summertime sanctuary. In keeping my promise to Brian to return to my roots as an athlete, I showed up in central Oregon, armed with a new road bike that my father had purchased for me as a graduation present, ready to get back in touch with being an endurance athlete. Matt, Matt, and I had arrived, again with several friends, all sharing the hope of finding more sustainable employment and to live in a town that began to feel like a home.

Heading southwest from Bend, on Century Drive, toward Mount Bachelor Ski Resort, lay the resort of The Inn of the Seventh Mountain. I was employed there the previous four summers, working banquets and server shifts at the '80s-clad facility. During those periods of employment, I, along with several of my buddies, Matt and Matt included, set up shop at the Inn to deprive the place of any innocence it might once have had. Over those summers, the Inn became a place that we used as a home base of sorts. For those years, the Inn was where we worked, partied, ate, sunbathed, swam, slept, and partied some more. Those times pulled us together in a deep bond.

Legend has it that the Inn was constructed over an Indian burial ground. For that reason, it seemed to be jinxed from the get-go. By the time my friends and I rolled into town, the Inn had undergone four bankruptcies since the time it was built in 1972. Around Bend, the resort had acquired the nickname of "Inn of the 11th Chapter." Fortunately, by the summer of 2002, a new management team had been brought in to revamp the image of the place. The Inn's survival depended on a much-needed change in leadership and millions of dollars in renovations. Many of the lodging units still featured shag carpet, vestiges of the mid-twentieth century. It was rumored that several pornography movies had been filmed in some of the rooms decades beforehand. Obviously, the Inn was long overdue for a facelift.

———

The kick start to revamping myself into an athlete was largely fostered by my new obsession with road biking. Over the last year at college, by the time graduation hit, a gain in sixty pounds of body fat had damaged me. My road bike and I teamed up to peel off the weight by putting in the miles. Within a month of being back in Bend, riding every single day had become a habit. Each successive day on the bike, I could feel my endurance coming back, and I was reminded of the physical and mental sensations of becoming fit. Within two months of solid riding, I paired up with my buddy Ben and rode my first century (one hundred miles) all the way from Bend to Mount Hood. That feat symbolized a significant milestone for me; I felt like I had finally resumed being an endurance athlete. Road cycling and I are partners; the partnership has lasted eighteen years.

Apart from biking, as the summer of 2002 progressed, my ambition to make a life for myself grew. I wasn't quite sure how I'd get a full-time, big-boy job, but I knew that Bend was inviting me to live there for a while. Toward the end of that summer, Davis Smith, the Inn's director of sales and marketing, approached me out of the blue. Apparently he had been keeping an eye on my work ethic over the previous two months that I worked at the Inn, impressed by my ability to forge relationships with several of the resort guests as well as with my coworkers. I had made such an impression on him that he wanted to know if I had ever considered a career in hospitality, more specifically in a sales and marketing capacity. I had never really considered career like that. I figured that I would probably follow up my psychology degree from SLU with a master's program somewhere. Even though Davis and I did not get close over the summer, I knew that he seemed like a grade-A, legit guy and could become a potential role model for me. Desiring a sustainable lifestyle, or simply feeling wanted, after a few hours of intense consideration, I agreed to interview with him and his sales team for placement as a team member.

To my surprise, he offered me the job. Holy shit, I thought, I have a full-time job! I was the first among my peers in Bend to land substantial employment. Pride began to settle in.

I couldn't believe that I had spent the last year and a half completely fucking off at college to the point where I had to cheat to graduate, only to be the first of my friends to be offered a full-time gig. Rather than being modest and unassuming with my first real job, I immediately elevated myself to being better than everyone else, more accomplished, and more apt to succeed. The fact that someone had shown an interest in my talents and abilities, from a professional standpoint, meant that I was superior to my peers. "Look out, world, I'm coming into my own." I was off and running with my new lifestyle because, well, I fucking deserved it. Look at me, I thought. I can fuck up badly and still come out on top. That was the first time in my life that I felt invincible. Little did I know that invincibility would become a derogatory common thread as my life unfolded.

My friend and mentor, Davis Smith, 2012

Davis took me to the Portland Ski Show in early November of 2002 to initiate my sales and marketing training. For anyone who has not been at a trade show before, it's a chance for a company to showcase its products to thousands of potential customers in a limited three-day time span.

After putting together our display booth and preparing for the opening of the show, he calmly mentioned that "it was time to see what I was made of." He wanted to see that his new recruit was going to pay off. Gulp.

That first day of the trade show, people would come up to me in the booth and ask questions; I had no idea what I was talking about. Each time a question was posed about the resort, it must have been apparent that I was clueless as to what I was promoting. I even got a few odd glances and signals from Davis; I surmised that he had obviously made a mistake in hiring me. Thankfully, my luck was about to change. Once trade shows approach closing time for the day, all of the vendors start drinking. With that, Davis fetched a few beers from our cooler, and I began to loosen up. Drinking beer injected me with the ease necessary for talking with the visitors to our booth. This was similar to how I felt during my first week as a freshman at college. I felt more comfortable chatting and talking about the Inn, and I even had the gumption to seek out other vendors to show them my skills as a gregarious extrovert.

As the last hour of that day progressed, a certain familiar fire reignited right underneath my feet. Even with just a few beers in me, I realized that I could actually be good at this job—that I could talk to people that I didn't even know. "Hell yes, this is perfect." I'm being paid to drink! That day, the pairing of alcohol along with the sales and marketing world would clearly define itself. And so it began: phase two of my relationship with alcohol was closing in. Not only was I able to practice what I had learned at St. Lawrence in terms of partying, but I was going to make money doing it. A freaking annual salary, in fact. I was winning!

———

I had an absolute blast working at the Inn for the next two years. Over time, Davis and I grew to be close friends. At every opportunity, he would bring me along to meetings to keep me in the loop on his projects. He had unofficially become the professional mentor in my life. After he felt comfortable enough with me around his buddies and family, the real fun began. Davis believed that I was trustworthy, not just as a business associate but also as a friend. His influence over me was and is actively profound.

Professionally, Davis taught me how to sell shit, how to talk on the phone, how to schmooze, how to play the game, and how to be a pro in the business world. He made it all look so easy, and when we were together, his presence alone gave me confidence. I tried to emulate his style. I eventually came to want what he had: a beautiful wife, a great house, gorgeous kids, and an unbeatable charm. Davis taught me to grow up, to be responsible, and to believe in myself.

Davis also introduced me to the Oregon State University Beavers athletic teams. As a graduate of OSU, he was obsessed with everything having to do with the Beavs. See, in Oregon, if you're new to the area, you have a very important and unavoidable decision to make. It's similar to living in New England. You're either a Red Sox fan or you're a Yankees fan. I had to make the choice early on living in the Beaver state. Was I going to be a Beavers fan or follow the Ducks? Eugene was home to the Oregon Ducks at the University of Oregon, while the Beavers were in Corvallis. I knew nothing about either town. At first I thought that I might be a Duck for the simple reason that their colors were the same as the Oakland Athletics, green and yellow. Plus, my first new car, purchased when I was hired at the Inn, was a green Volkswagen Jetta, so it made sense that I'd lean toward being a Duck. However, that notion was quickly shot down by Davis. As in completely squashed. He made it clear from the get-go that if I was going to work for and be friends with him, I didn't have a choice. Therefore I declared myself a dedicated Beavers fan. End of story.

During my first full fall in Bend, Davis was able to pull a trifecta in Beaver football game-day experiences. In the 2003 season, I went to three Beavers games at Reser Stadium, their home territory. I sat in the press box during the first game, the stands during the second game, and for the third game, I was on the sidelines next to the team. It was a thrill to be connected with a new sports team to follow rather than just focusing my attention on my beloved A's. The college football scene presented another familiar form of engagement: full-on raging tailgate parties that lasted all day. These parties sparked memories of days at SLU. Things were really coming together.

College game day in Corvallis was hard to beat. Throughout the day leading up to kickoff, parties were everywhere. And I mean everywhere. On a typical home-game weekend, forty-five thousand fans congregated from all over the Northwest in Corvallis to watch their Beavers and to get hammered. Tailgate parties stretched for miles; people walked up and down the streets of town with open containers of beer, liquor, and wine. Corvallis seemed to incorporate the lawlessness of Las Vegas, where the open container law doesn't exist. I wanted a piece of this atmosphere for myself. Having foresight, Davis would get us hotel rooms for the night so that we could clown around town after the game and party like we were college kids. I could blend in easily with the students because I had just graduated from college. The entire game-day experience each time we went to Corvallis that fall was an absolute blast.

My coworkers at the Inn were amazing as well. Cheryl and Anne, senior members of the sales team, became like my big sisters, helping and coaching me through several professional situations that were completely foreign to me. Both women provided the perfect complement to Davis's style of training. Since I really was ignorant of the proper tactics in building a sales team, Davis asked me to sit in and participate in an interview for a new position he was filling. We were hiring for an additional sales position. Whatever was going to help me learn, I was ready to experience. What I didn't know was that the person I was about to help interview would end up having a huge impact on my life further down the road. Her name was Vanessa, and she was gorgeous.

During the interview, I couldn't keep my shit together. I was less interested in how she might fit with the team and more interested in just getting to know her. I seriously could not stop staring at her. I must've sounded like a blithering idiot trying to put together interview questions. The minute we started talking, however, I knew exactly how this was going to play out. She'd get hired, and we'd end up dating. I knew it. And as luck would have it, after Vanessa was hired, we began to form a friendship right off the bat.

My relationship with Vanessa was different. Up until the point we started dating, I was used to immature relationships with college girls. I really didn't know anything else. Apart from Hillary, during freshman and sophomore year at SLU, I had not been in any type of significant relationship. I was eager to call Vanessa my girlfriend and be a part of a big-boy partnership. I felt grown up.

Having a real job, a new car, and a new life, I was thrilled to date someone who had recently entered the professional world as well. Perhaps we could wade through this exciting world together?

Unfortunately, it wasn't meant to be. After a few short months of dating, Vanessa and I thought it would be best to split. It was awkward at work at first, but as time went on, our friendship continued, which would ultimately prove valuable down the road.

Meanwhile, I was becoming really damn good at my job. I became a chronic overachiever of sorts. I made more prospecting calls, hosted more site tours, and set up more client meetings than anyone on our team. My pride was fed with each step of progress. Having Davis by my side during this time was a tremendous help. He gave me confidence in ways that even he couldn't fathom. He had replaced the big-brother role that used to belong to Matt and Matt.

Davis would also include me in his happy-hour gatherings with his select group of thirty-something-year-old friends whom I viewed as *the* players in town at the time. I made that assessment mostly due to the fact that Super-Bowl-winning NFL legend Drew Bledsoe was included in the crowd. My assumption was that anyone who hung around Drew must be a big deal. Plus, all of these guys had what I wanted: a wife, a house, the cars, and the money. I would do whatever it took to fit in with this group of guys. Fortunately for me, their world seemed to largely revolve around daily happy-hour cocktails. Wait a minute! I thought. I fucking know how to play this game! Back at SLU, I had mastered the craft of getting to know everyone and having them like me. Fuck, I was the president of my fraternity! Maybe now I could become the mayor of Bend!

Gradually, Bend seemed like it was becoming the ideal place to implement the skills I had learned in the latter stages of college. My minor in excessive alcohol abuse at St. Lawrence could come in handy in the professional world. I was pumped.

In continuing to keep my promise to Brian, I faithfully pursued training. I began doing strength sessions three days per week, along with riding six to seven times per week. The following winter I even got back on my cross-country skis and ventured out on the trails my friends and I used to hit over the summer during college. As a consequence, I was getting skinnier, leaner, and more attractive (to me, anyway). I didn't necessarily believe that I could get back into an endurance sport like cross-country skiing, but maybe I could be good at *something* again. For the first time in a long while, from an athletic perspective, my hope to regain the confidence I had back when I was on top of my game and racing with top junior skiers in the country was reachable.

Cycling continued to take hold of my personal life; professionally, I was seeing continued progress in my ability to create and forge business relationships within the central Oregon community. Life was looking pretty fucking good for me. I found myself feeling like I had made it professionally, personally, athletically, and even emotionally. Ah, yes, more invincibility.

With the combination of athletics and my job backing me up, I forged ahead into the mid-2000s. After being recruited to join a competing property, Eagle Crest Resort, as a twenty-four-year-old director of sales (a rarity for my age in the resort business), I also stepped up my game with cycling. By 2005, I had successfully put together one of the largest and most successful amateur cycling teams in the state of Oregon, along with working my way to a competitive Category 3 racer on the road. I was kicking ass in every way possible. It even got to the point where I put my first offer in on a house.

The central Oregon real estate market was going bananas in those years, so I took my salary and leveraged it into a piece of the dream that I had so thoroughly sought since meeting Davis and his friends. I so wanted what they all had! By August of 2005, I was finally financially capable of having a home built; the only missing link was the girl.

Then, one afternoon at work, I got an e-mail from my friend Heather. The subject line simply read, "There's someone I think you should meet."

CHAPTER 12

Fall 2010

*B*am, bam, bam!

As I shook off a hangover haze, resulting from another stout night of partying in downtown Bend, I opened my apartment front door to find Jeff yelling at me to get out of bed. This was certainly a role reversal, as I was normally the one to wake his ass up. Jeff is notorious for sleeping in, sometimes until 11:00 a.m. or noon, on his days off from work. "Fuck, that's right!" We were heading to Corvallis for the game today! It was 7:00 a.m. Arizona State University was coming to Corvallis to play the Beavers.

Jeff's infectious enthusiasm quickly reminded me that it was going to be a great day because, well, every college football game day is a great day. After scrambling to find some suitable game-day gear, I dragged myself into Jeff's car to begin our pilgrimage to see our beloved Beavers. By the time we reached Sisters, Oregon, roughly twenty minutes outside of Bend, I was already on my way to getting fucked up. Jeff had come prepared with a bottle of Knob Creek for us to indulge in throughout the day. I opened it immediately and poured some into my cup of coffee. What Jeff didn't know was that during the previous night, I was able to score some Ritalin (similar to Adderall, Ritalin is another prescription pill that people use to manage

ADHD). By the time we reached Sisters, the pills I had taken before getting in his car were already taking effect.

Jeff was keenly aware that I was into excessive drinking. He was gaining insight into what I was capable of drinking by myself. He therefore strategically picked up another bottle of whiskey to have on hand so that he could have some for himself.

Two hours later, we rolled into Corvallis. It was 9:30 a.m., and I was fucking hammered. By that point, I had guzzled most of the Knob Creek and some of the contents of the second whiskey bottle (unbeknown to Jeff), essentially leaving Jeff with the pack of Coors Light that we had brought with us. Thankfully, we were going to meet up with some of Jeff's OSU pharmacy school buddies at a tailgater, so our alcohol problem was more or less solved for the day. We knew they'd be fully stocked and loaded. By 11:30 a.m., the bottle of Knob Creek was gone. Mix in some gravity beer bongs, a few lines of chopped-up Ritalin, and Jell-O shots, and I was well on my way to making it another great game day. I had even managed to force a few hot dogs down my throat to help take the edge off of my insane buzz. At around 12:30 p.m., we wrapped up the tailgater and started to make our way to the game.

By that time, I was so fucked up that while walking from our parking spot at the rugby fields, the world began to spin out of control. My vision was becoming warped; my mind was in the gutter. Somehow I successfully made my way into the game. I don't remember kickoff.

"Spence! Spence! Where the fuck are you?"

The loud screams calling my name were unbearable. I had passed out in the driver's seat of Jeff's car.

"Where the fuck did you go?" said Jeff.

"Dude, I don't know, what quarter is it?" I replied.

"The game's over. It was sick! Dude, I can't believe you missed it!"

"Seriously, man, what the fuck are you talking about?" I said.

I had missed the entire game.

As Jeff tells the story, I did make it into Reser Stadium that day, but within minutes, I was on my way back out, staying for less than three minutes to cheer on our Beavers. Somehow, in a complete blackout, I had safely made my way back to our parking spot and into Jeff's car. I have no idea what route I took.

"How the hell are we going to get back home? I'm fucking hammered!" said Jeff.

I didn't know. The best thing that came to mind was to finish the remainder of the second bottle of whiskey to catch my second wind, and then I'd drive us back to Bend. Ritalin could help get me straight. Within ten minutes, we had hit the road home, and I was driving.

Reaching the tiny little town of Sweet Home just forty minutes later, we decided it would be a good idea to down more cocktails and food at a dive bar not far from the highway. Rather than drinking water to help sober up for the car ride to my apartment, we chose to drink more whiskey. Revived, we got back into the car and finished the ninety-minute drive back to Bend. How I managed to stay on my side of the road without killing anyone, or ourselves, for that matter, is a mystery.

Once safely home, I stumbled into my apartment feeling exceedingly guilty for what I had just done. There was no pride or invincibility to reassure me on this day. I had driven us back from Corvallis, a little more than a two-hour drive, after blacking out, waking up, and getting hammered again. As I sat on my couch that night feeling sorry for myself, I remembered the extra stash of Ritalin in my kitchen cabinet. Without hesitation, I chopped up the pills, grabbed some beers, snorted the Ritalin, shot-gunned the beers, and made my way back to downtown Bend by myself to get the ball rolling again.

The next morning, I woke up in another fog. I didn't know how I had gotten home from another night of partying in Bend. With a pounding headache, I started to piece together what I had achieved the previous day. I'd ingested Ritalin and Knob Creek, driven the car, taken Jell-O shots, guzzled down beer bongs, drank more whiskey, gone to a football game (sort of), had more beers and Ritalin, driven the car again, snorted yet more lines of Ritalin, and, finally, capped it all off with more whiskey shots somewhere in downtown Bend.

Holy fucking shit, I thought. I could have died yesterday. I could have driven off the road with my best friend in the passenger seat and killed him! What the fuck was I thinking? Simply put, I wasn't thinking.

CHAPTER 13

Beyond excited, I responded to Heather's e-mail within seconds. "Hell yeah, Heather, I'm game." And so began the end of my life as I knew it. No experience I had ever had up to this point could have prepared me for what was about to happen.

Lauren's first e-mail to me read something like this: "Hi, my name is Lauren. I cook, clean, love dogs, and am supposedly the last girl you'll ever have to talk to." Perhaps it was her way of showing some witty, sophisticated humor. It worked.

The bait Lauren dangled in front of me came at the perfect time. Heather had met Lauren through a mutual friend in Philadelphia. Heather lived in Washington, DC; Lauren was living in the outskirts of Philadelphia, working as an administrative assistant and as an assistant swimming coach at a local high school academy. The two girls connected through the competitive swimming world. Lauren was a lifelong swimmer and associated with the Hansen family (Sean and Brendan, the latter being a three-time Olympian). Brendan competed with guys like Michael Phelps, Ryan Lochte, Aaron Piersol (an athlete I've just recently grown to admire for his approach to sport), and many others. He had already won an Olympic gold medal. Heather had a crush on Brendan. So Heather and Lauren became close friends.

After her initial e-mail, Lauren and I began to exchange e-mails all day, every day. At the time, I was crushing it in my job as director of sales at Eagle Crest Resort, working for my buddy TJ, who had recruited me away from working for Davis at the Inn of the Seventh Mountain. Throughout Lauren's and my communication, we learned a lot about each other. She had sent me a picture of Heather and herself, posing. I was immediately attracted to her. Lauren fell into the physical mold that I was in pursuit of: blond, skinny, and a great tan. We also had a mutual love of Mötley Crüe. Eventually the e-mails turned into daily phone calls. I could carry on a great conversation with her. By the time August rolled around, we decided that we should meet. We had interacted with each other for two months only verbally, so it seemed like the next logical step in our relationship. Without hesitation, I immediately booked a plane ticket back east. I figured that I had nothing to lose. Perhaps she was the one, and I wanted to find out.

Lauren met me as I exited the Philadelphia airport terminal. The minute she saw me, she began to hop up and down, subtly clapping her hands in excitement. I knew it—I had found the one. Within seconds of meeting her, I started to plan our wedding in my head. This was perfect. I had my life laid out in front of me. Along with making wedding plans, I was already plotting to move back east, start a family with my hot blond wife, and live happily ever after. As we walked out of the airport together, I knew that I had owned the day and won.

Our first visit together was exhilarating. We spent a couple of days at Heather's house on Cape Cod. Surrounded by yacht-club dudes and their hot wives all weekend, I was convinced that I had made it to the top; I was going to be able to wear Ralph Lauren polo shirts, sip fine whiskey, smoke cigars, and mingle with New England's most elite and important *twenty-something*-year-olds. This group shimmered with shitloads of money, and I wanted my share of its glow.

After leaving the Cape, Lauren and I made our way up to Manchester, New Hampshire, to see our beloved Mötley Crüe rock the shit out of a concert stadium. Two days later, while staying at a hotel adjacent to the Manchester airport so that she could catch a flight back to Philadelphia the next day, we hung out in the hot tub and played in the pool.

That evening carved out an indelible memory in my mind. As she was prancing from the pool to join me in the hot tub, I caught a glimpse of her that more or less sealed our fate. She looked adorable in her petite body, almost like a well-honed cross-country skier. I decided right then and there that I was going to marry Lauren.

When I returned to Bend, I stayed in touch with Lauren several times a day; then, another professional development in my life began to surface.

What if someone told you in a job interview that if you were offered the job, you would make up to $500K in your first year? As an ambitious and money-hungry twenty-six-year-old, would you take it if it were offered to you? Fuck yeah, you would.

As the director of sales at Eagle Crest Resort, under the flag of Jeld-Wen communities, I had a leg up on hearing about new job opportunities that surfaced within the company. The central Oregon real estate market in late 2005 was going fucking bonkers. Truly, it was flat-out ridiculous. Since 2002, the Bend housing market was seeing a 20–22 percent increase in value year over year, or so I was led to believe. I witnessed, firsthand, friends of mine who owned homes make $100K in equity in one year due to the appreciation in the market. Broker friends were killing it, bringing home commission checks in one month that put my yearly salary to shame. It was a time of "funny money" in Bend, and the idea of forfeiting this opportunity was eating away at me.

I had the girl, the car, and the house; now I wanted the real money. Forget this meager director-of-sales salary; I deserved more. After conferring with a friend who was on the ground floor at Jeld-Wen's premier golf resort, located just a few miles outside of Bend, I put my name in the ring to be interviewed for the resort's real estate sales team. My friend had indicated that I should keep my expectations low, as close to one hundred other people were applying for the same position. With luck on my side, I was granted an interview. I knew with every fiber in my body that if I could get an interview, then I would get the job. Two days later, after killing it in the interview, the position was offered to me.

With word of the good news, I immediately called my mom. At that time, she was struggling financially. With my new job and the promise of several hundred thousand dollars on its way in the next year, I assured her that everything was going to be fine. Without even having earned a single paycheck, I was already proposing that I would buy her house so that she could have extra cash to live on. Some of my guaranteed riches were going to be invested in a condo in Oakland—so that I could go watch my beloved A's whenever I desired—and one on the Oregon coast as well.

The second call went to Lauren. Knowing that I was about to become loaded in the next couple of years, I proposed that she move to Oregon to live with me while I made money. Then, once I struck it rich, we could move back east so that we could set up the rest of our lives and be geographically closer to our friends and family. It was the perfect plan. She agreed.

In December of 2005, I closed on a house that was custom built for me earlier in the year. The cost to build the house was $196K. With Lauren's impending arrival in Bend in just a matter of weeks, I picked up the keys to our new home. The plan was materializing. While I worked my ass off getting paid, Lauren would be able to use some of the money I earned to reinvest in the house so that when we sold it, we'd clear at least $350,000, given the projections of the real estate market at the time. See, very few people seemed to believe that the Bend market was a bubble. In my new job, I was taught to tell potential clients that a bubble only happens when there are huge spikes in the market year over year. I was led to believe that the 20 percent YOY growth would be sustainable, simply due to the plain and simple fact that everyone wanted to move to Bend.

And so it began: my great new shiny job selling high-end golf course real estate with panoramic mountain views of the Oregon Cascades. I was hell-bent on putting every shred of energy into keeping the promises that I made to my mom, to Lauren, and to myself. I wanted what my buddies in New York City had made for themselves; I wanted to actually be a fucking millionaire. With mere hope in hand, I felt more invincible than ever.

The winter of 2006 began with a bang. Lauren and I spent New Year's Eve in New York City with several of her friends and mine, including Jeff and Brian. God, it felt good to be around the guys who I looked up to as financially successful. I would soon be one of them, a player in the money game. With Lauren having permanently relocated to Oregon in February of 2006, our life together finally commenced. I started to live my dream.

Almost immediately, I started pounding the proverbial pavement to take advantage of the thriving real estate market conditions. Seventy- to eighty-hour workweeks were habitual. The days were filled with making hundreds of prospecting calls to compete with the other brokers in the office and trying to be the best and most committed broker in the group. I took my learned skills of being an overachiever at the Inn of the Seventh Mountain and Eagle Crest Resort and applied them to a job where I could make ten times more money. It was the perfect storm to make my financial mark on the world. I was the "young buck," eager and ambitious to impress the hell out of my bosses so that they would reassure me that I was the best broker on staff. I built an ego the size of California by way of the encouragement of my bosses, who said that if I kept up this level of activity, I could be the King of Bend, a "player" in the central Oregon scene. Hell yeah, this sounded too good to be true.

Blinded by the illusion of striking it rich, I was forced to let one priority in my life go: fitness. By the summer of 2006, I had only ridden my bike a couple of times that year. Undertaking any physical activity took a back seat to my job. The cycling team that I had started a few years prior dropped completely off my radar. Long weekend group rides became a thing of the past. Without really noticing, my fitness disappeared just like it had after I had quit the ski team at St. Lawrence. Once again, I really didn't care, because money became the priority—wads and wads of cash.

Throughout 2006, money evolved as an addiction. On the home front, Lauren was mysteriously beginning to isolate herself and withdraw from me. I vaguely understood, partly because she didn't have many friends in Bend. But something else was going on, and I didn't really understand it. I believed that I was treating her well, taking her to expensive restaurants and on shopping trips when I had a day off, but she was not responding to me like she used to. Her isolation drove her to bed by 5:00 p.m. most afternoons, even in the summer when everyone in Bend was playing outdoors. The money I threw at her prompted her to momentarily snap out of her funk. But just as quickly as she would seem happy, she would inevitably retreat to her isolation.

Over that summer, we began to get into fights, not physical but verbally abusive and emotionally driven. As a spectator to her habitual withdrawal, I, of course, wanted to fix it. I started doing and saying things that would hopefully appease her depressive state and make her feel happy, like I had tried to do with my mom when I was a kid. When my intentions failed, I would take it personally, and down the rabbit hole we would jump, as a couple, straight into self-loathing and inexorable confusion. At the end of the day, all I cared about was if she was happy or not. I started to feel trapped.

Meanwhile, at work, the momentum continued to build from my efforts. The hard work was beginning to pay off because the real estate market remained hot. Even though I was the youngest broker, I was making vast inroads into the circle of trust of my supervisors. My physical health, however, continued to decline. In order to deal with the frustration that I was having with Lauren, I regressed into bad habits.

Some evenings, I found myself making pit stops at a country store in the tiny town of Alfalfa on my way home from work. At first I would pick up something inconsequential, like a can of Coors Light, to sip on the way home. This sneaky little trick would help me cope with Lauren's inevitable withdrawal that I was about to face at home. Within a month of starting this habit, I began to drink on the way home every evening. As Lauren's mood worsened, I surrendered to alcohol to numb my anxiety.

By late 2006, I was consuming three twenty-two-ounce cans of CAMO XXX malt liquor on my way home. I mean, this was absolute shit beer; I might as well have mixed swamp water with gasoline and tossed it down. I didn't even care about the taste; I wanted the effect. These disgraceful beers contained 12.8 percent alcohol. In my opinion, the more alcohol content, the better. Anything that could slow down my senses in dealing with an unavoidable mess at home was OK with me.

One night at dinner, fueled up with my now normal postwork alcohol concoctions, I gathered up the nerve to open up to Lauren about my concerns with my own health. Over peach Bellinis at Bend's old Staccato restaurant, I expressed my desire to get back into bike racing. I had gained sixty pounds since the spring of 2005 when my racing weight was 170. I felt disgusting, fat, and lethargic. And I looked like shit.

The conversation went like this:

Me: "I think I would like to get back into shape and return to bike racing. I feel disgusting."

Lauren: "Why would you want to do that?"

Me: "Because I was happier when I felt fit."

Lauren: "Why? We both know what happens when you get athletic. You pay more attention to yourself than to me. Besides, I like fat Spencer better."

The "fat Spence" days, together with my friend Zach at his wedding in 2006

In order to circumvent another tiff between us, I took it in the balls and let it be. Making Lauren mad scared me. What I didn't realize was how her support of "Fat Spence" would come back later in life to haunt me. Needless to say, I didn't get back on my bike. Instead, it remained as it was, in my garage, covered in dust.

By New Year's Eve at the end of 2006 the situation between us had worsened. Excessive closet drinking was routine. Lauren was becoming more and more frustrated being in Oregon, three thousand miles away from her friends and family. We joined a couple of our close friends in NYC to ring in the New Year. It was a simple night with good food, good cocktails, and light conversation. Brian and Lauren were even having a good time chatting with each other, which, in my experience, was rare.

As the night moved on, we ended up at some random bar to celebrate the ball dropping in Times Square. I remember casually standing up and talking privately to Brian. During our one-on-one, a smoking-hot girl walked by, and I motioned to Brian that he should go talk to her. Well, that didn't set well with Lauren.

Assuming that I was the one eyeballing her, she immediately stood up and stormed out of the bar. Motherfucker, here we go again. How long could I keep doing this to myself? As I caught up to her in the street outside of where we were staying, it was clear that she had no interest in talking about what she assumed had happened. With my tail between my legs, I apologized, yet again, for something that resulted from *her* perception. Hell, I had no fucking clue what I had done! I had to follow through with my inevitable reaction to always make her happy, and I was really getting sick of it.

As we entered her friend's apartment, where we had arranged to stay for the night, Lauren maintained her stern and pissed-off look. My anxiety was mounting to an all-time high. Maybe this was my chance to do something that I should've done months ago: end this fucking disaster. Eject! Get out! Run the fuck away!

To catch my breath, I went into the bathroom to think about what should happen next. After ten minutes of feeling paranoid, I reached into my toiletry bag and pulled out the ring that my mother had given me to give to the woman I wanted to marry. I had the ring on me for a purpose, perhaps for a moment exactly like this. What the fuck? Really? Holding the ring, a carat-and-a-half diamond that once belonged to my great-grandmother, I thought about my options. Maybe proposing to Lauren was the answer to all of our problems. Maybe by letting her know, officially, that I was dedicated for the long term, I would vanquish her depression and make her happy again. Yes, that's it. That is the answer. Let's do this.

Two minutes later, I was down on one knee, asking Lauren to marry me. She said yes. Her anger went away in an instant. Satisfied that I had dodged another bullet, we began calling all of our friends and family to spread the news. It was 1:00 a.m. on January 1, 2007, and I was engaged.

Earlier in December, still in Oregon and preparing to leave for vacation, I had a very emotional conversation with Jeff about proposing to Lauren. We were hammered, pounding Coronas and whiskey, debating whether this idea was a good one. Actually, I was the only one debating myself about the idea. Jeff wasn't buying any of the shit that was coming out of my mouth, much less the faulty reasoning behind it. I defended my position for hours. Jeff got too drunk to tolerate the conversation any longer. At the end, in a slurred voice, he simply said that he supported me in whatever I chose to do. Talk about warning signs. One of my best friends was convinced that the idea of proposing to Lauren was a mistake. He simply hated the notion of us getting married.

Lauren and I went home to Bend after the holiday to settle back into our central Oregon life. Lauren seemed happier overall. At her instigation, we had started to plan our move to the East Coast together. I hadn't quite yet made all of the money that I had expected to make, so we set the date of arrival for January 2008, giving me a solid year to cash in my chips after exploiting the Bend-area real estate market. My business cohorts believed that the real estate market would continue to skyrocket. Otherwise I wouldn't have known any better. Playing even more to my advantage was the fact that all but one of the brokers from 2006 had left. My buddy Jeremy and I were now among the senior sales guys on the team, which meant that we had the opportunity to handpick clients who were potential buyers from the stockpile that the old team was handling. It was going to be a big year, and I was locked and loaded with motivation to get my piece of the pie. Time to sit back and watch the cash roll in.

Armed with new confidence and a happy fiancée, I began to make some personal financial decisions to prepare us for our departure the following year. When I purchased my house in 2005, it was appraised at $196K. One year later, it appraised for $320K. Rather than hold off on cashing in, I took every single penny out through a refinancing. Suddenly, I was *cash* rich. Lauren and I celebrated by buying her a new car; on top of that, we bought a huge big-screen TV and entertainment center. Then I paid for something known as a Frexel procedure, a $5,000 facial operation to remove wrinkles, something Lauren said she needed, three separate times.

The spending was reckless, but it didn't matter because my income in 2007 was going to soar. I wasn't even worried about the new loan I had taken out. It was an interest-only kind of deal, which still left me with plenty of extra cash to spend every month. The ARM (adjustable-rate mortgage) in the loan would balloon three years later, when I would have already sold my home for twice the value and purchased something impressive back east. No need for any worry. I had it figured out.

By the spring of 2007, Lauren and I seemed to be doing OK together. Work was still going well, and the market seemed to be holding steady as my bosses figured it would; well, at least that was what they said. The fights between Lauren and me were less frequent because she knew she was moving back east. That made her happy. She never really formed any long-lasting friendships on the West Coast. She had me, my house, and the money. Oh, and lest I forget...she also had the $800 pug I purchased for her. Then in June, shit started to get weird very quickly.

One day at work, Lauren called me. She had received a strange call earlier in the day from a private investigator. The PI was looking into some leads he had for his client, who was receiving vicious, abusive e-mails. What the fuck? Lauren didn't even know anyone, so why would she be involved in a case relating to someone in Bend getting weird e-mails?

After my own investigation, I discovered that the claims were filed by Vanessa, my good friend whom I dated and worked with at the Inn back in 2004. As the PI reported, Vanessa had been the victim of several harassing e-mails attacking her religious views, political views, and overall personality. She was going through an all-out character assassination. Vanessa thought Lauren and I were behind the attack, and she had taken matters into her own hands. Upon hearing this news, I was fucking dumbfounded. And totally pissed off.

Once the allegations had surfaced, Vanessa became a regular topic of our daily discussion. In fact, it was all Lauren wanted to talk about: how Vanessa was crazy, insane, and ridiculous for even considering her as a culprit. My frustration with the situation fostered resentment toward Vanessa; it didn't even cross my mind to go talk to her because I damn well knew that would have pissed off Lauren. Another fight was out of the question.

After a solid month of the constant back and forth between Lauren and me about how Vanessa was ruining our lives, I had had enough. The discussions were exhausting. Lauren was becoming obsessed with the situation. None of it made sense. In the meantime, Lauren decided that she was going to make her way back east earlier than planned to set up our next phase of life. She was scheduled to leave in the beginning of July. Her eventual departure switched her focus away from the whole rigmarole with Vanessa. Once Lauren left Oregon, the fiasco vanished.

On July 4th, I found myself in my house alone; Lauren was already on the road, crossing through Utah on her way back east. To celebrate my temporary freedom, I bought a fifth of whiskey, turned off my phone, and proceeded to slip into a blackout. I sat on my couch that night, watching the Pacino/De Niro film *Heat*, pounding whiskey, and feeling sorry for myself and my situation. The next morning when I awoke, sixteen text messages and nine missed calls were recorded on my phone. For once, I didn't care about the repercussions that I'd have to endure from missing all of

Lauren's calls and not responding. I relished being by myself, physically, for the first time in over a year.

---◦◦◦---

I wouldn't be alone for long. My friend Brian, seeking a life change of his own, decided that he would move to Bend for a few months to be with me until it was time for me to drive across the country to begin my new life. Brian was a big golfer, so he was excited to check out all of the well-known central Oregon courses. His presence there would soon prove to be a life-saver, literally.

As July turned into August, the word was out that the real estate market, even in nonstop 20-percent-gain-YOY Bend, was slowing down. It had been a slower summer than we had originally projected from a sales standpoint, but not for a long enough time for anyone to start panicking. Just as soon as my bosses indicated that we would be fine—because the high-end golf resort property market was not subject to the laws of normal residential areas—the bottom fell out, and the market began to crash. The subprime mortgage crisis began to hit the ground in central Oregon, destroying people's financial health by crushing the equity in their investments.

Speculation in the market, the trend over the last five years, began to wipe out everything for everybody. In what seemed like the blink of an eye, the game of foreclosure became a new, exciting hobby—everyone was doing it. In Bend, the new sport was dropping your house keys off at the bank and telling the bank to fuck off. People were losing everything, and I may as well have been the poster child.

I was less concerned about Lauren and more concerned about how the fuck I was going to survive financially. The promise of being a rich real estate tycoon? Gone. Loads of equity in my house (or what was left of it)? Gone. Savings accounts? Gone. I had been sucked into the game that everyone else was playing, speculating on the market and leveraging myself to the hilt, and I was losing.

The crash in the market influenced my plan to relocate with Lauren. In just a matter of days, I had nothing—no cash, no equity, nothing. I only had an overpriced house full of expensive and useless furniture. Barely cognizant of this financial strain, Lauren started to accuse me of intentionally never making all the money that I had promised her. She said that I couldn't be trusted, that I was a phony. In one of these phone conversations, Lauren revealed that she found out that I had actually seen Vanessa at a BBQ earlier in the summer. Given the treacherous circumstances, Lauren might as well have assumed that I was cheating on her.

After that particular conversation, I threw my phone against a door, punched and kicked the wall, grabbed a bottle of Percocet and a bottle of wine, and decided to end my life. I couldn't fucking take it anymore. I was done. I had no energy left to contend with my problems. Lauren was driving me bat-shit crazy, and life was not worth living anymore. Luckily, before I could act on my desperate straits, Brian found me curled up in the fetal position in my stairwell, sobbing uncontrollably. Brian had just saved my life.

———∞∞∞———

My first stint at Sageview Psychiatric Center, Bend's inpatient hospital for people with mental health issues and suicidal tendencies, began.

For one week, I was housed within the concrete walls of Sageview with all sorts of characters: meth addicts, schizophrenics, drunks, and denizens of skid row, the lowest of the low. Relinquishing any communication with the outside world, I was forced to look at my life through a different lens, one that I didn't really care to use.

After a few days of being in Sageview, I called my mom, my dad, and Lauren to let them know what was going on. All three were scared shitless for me, but the sentiments didn't reach me. I was too consumed with my problems to acknowledge any of their concerns. In the back of my mind, I was secretly savoring the fact that Lauren had to stop being a bitch and focus on my health for a change.

Within a couple of days, the psychiatrists at Sageview officially diagnosed my condition as depression. This diagnosis had been a long time coming. Initially the doctors thought I might have been bipolar, but after a series of psychiatric tests, the results showed I was suffering only from depression, exacerbated by the effects of my addiction to shitty-ass malt liquor.

More than anything else, my stay at Sageview was a reprieve from my chaotic life. It felt good to be disconnected from Lauren and the heartache and trouble she had been causing me. My stay at Sageview was like a vacation. I learned that I did not have the stamina for the fast-paced atmosphere that had consumed me over the past two years. Although my job wasn't the whole problem, it certainly was not helping matters.

When the doctors released me, they ordered me to stop drinking and to start taking a daily dose of antidepressants. I immediately called my boss and let her know that I was coming in to see her. Without going into details on where I had been the past week, I wished her well and resigned from my job. No two-week notice and no good-byes, merely a quiet, quick exit.

As I left my office that day, a sense of failure overcame me. What had I accomplished here? Based on false promises, I had made very little money, leveraged myself as high as I could go, and lost everything in the process.

Within two weeks of leaving my job, I had sold everything in my house, closed all my bank accounts, and prepared to leave for the East Coast, hardly the way in which I planned. No equity, no money, no self-confidence, a bruised-as-fuck ego, and a depressing fiancée awaiting my early arrival. I had also become a complete fat-ass. Everything that I had attempted to achieve when I first landed my big-boy, big-money job never came to fruition. There was no million-dollar payday at the end of the rainbow. I felt more lost than ever.

Baltimore, Maryland. That was the city where we decided to start over. Baltimore fucking Maryland. I had absolutely no idea what I had been thinking when I agreed to change coasts. The one and only thing that I was looking forward to in Baltimore was that the Oakland A's visited to play the Orioles for three games per year. The prospect of making Baltimore my next home fueled my depression. Miraculously, most likely due to Brian's company, I didn't drink once during those last two weeks in Bend. I didn't even say good-bye to anyone, other than Davis, before I left.

"Welcome to Maryland" the sign read. Uh, yeah, fuck that. What the fuck am I doing here? I thought. While cruising down from Massachusetts—my cat, Bailey, who had survived the drive across the country, was now staying with my mom—I took note of the landscape on either side of Interstate 93. This looked nothing like Oregon, and I was heartbroken.

As soon as I crossed into the Baltimore city limits, I was immediately struck by the feeling that something wasn't right. While paying no heed to my gut, my reunion with Lauren in this city didn't make any sense to me. Within a few days of being there, I was able to secure a job selling insurance. Selling insurance was the least sexy and least glamorous job that I could think of, especially after my career in high-end real estate.

"You're not ready to be married, Spencer" were the words in the e-mail. Lauren and I were in the midst of planning our wedding at a resort in Pennsylvania, so the idea of getting hitched was keenly on my mind. Unbeknown to me, my mother had been slowly building disdain for my relationship with Lauren. When reading the e-mail, I felt exceedingly guilty. For what, I did not know or understand. Later that day, I got a frantic call from Lauren.

"Did you see the e-mail your mom sent?" she asked.

"I did. I don't really know what to say," I replied.

"Well, what the fuck does she mean?"

"I don't know," I said in utter confusion.

After a few moments of processing this question, I suddenly realized that my mother had sent the e-mail to my personal Hotmail account. Wait a minute—how the hell did Lauren see the e-mail? I was perplexed. Ultimately, I let it slide; questioning Lauren would make her even more upset. Anything to keep Lauren happy! Geez. After a couple of days, the issue seemed to have blown over. But it would only be a matter of a few more days before the next crisis came about.

Another frantic phone call came through from Lauren while I was at work.

"I'm pregnant, Spence."

"Um, what? Holy fucking shit."

All at once, I became more terrified than ever. Ever!

"I had a pregnancy test done, and I'm several weeks pregnant."

The idea of being a father took a few days to settle in. I did not know how to comprehend the situation. What the fuck was I going to do? What were *we* going to do? My solution this time, while Lauren made a trip to her parents' house, was to go to some dive bar in Towson, Maryland, the Baltimore suburb we chose for our temporary home, and get absolutely shit-faced by myself. Once I had reached Maryland, I hadn't had too many chances to drink because Lauren was holding me accountable for what the doctors had prescribed back in Bend. I took the opportunity with grace to disregard any of her accountability bullshit and proceeded to numb out.

After mulling over my current circumstance for a few days by myself, I came to the conclusion that I was destined to be fucked for life. *Fucked for life.* I wasn't ready to be a father. In many ways I was still a child myself. How was this going to work? After three days of drinking in isolation, I accepted the fact that I was about to be married to a woman for whom I had no feelings and with whom I was going to have a child.

A few weeks later, after reality had sunk in, Lauren and I were on the verge of shopping for Christmas presents that we clearly could not afford. Before leaving the driveway, she mentioned that she didn't feel good and needed to go back inside for a second. I didn't think much of the complaint. After ten minutes, she returned to the car with a solemn and subdued look on her face. Lauren had just had a miscarriage. I didn't know how to respond.

Since arriving in Baltimore three months prior, I didn't even know which way was up. Strangled with anguish and disgust, I found myself not being able to breathe. Relentless anxiety was creeping in. Life was becoming more and more chaotic each day. My relationship with Lauren was worse than it had ever been, and I didn't have any idea what to do.

Putting the devastation of her miscarriage aside, Lauren and I made our way back to Worthington to join my mom for Christmas. The plan was to spend a few nights in Massachusetts with my mom and a few nights in Pennsylvania with Lauren's family, and then we'd make our way down to Philadelphia to link up with Jeff, who was visiting his parents. Overall, the trip was pleasant.

During a gathering with Lauren's family, which was mainly composed of women, I made the excuse that I wanted to watch a football game downstairs. Having been given the go-ahead, I made my way to her aunt's basement, found a bottle of Jack Daniels, and got shit-faced by myself. That episode was the highlight of my holidays.

Once we wrapped up doing the family thing, we made the three-hour drive to Philly to see Jeff. I found myself being silent during the drive; Lauren had become irritated with me for some unspecified reason. No surprise there. With our silence, my anxiety began to build. After two hours, we broke the silence and started to argue about some irrelevant, ridiculous issue. The debate then turned into a passive-aggressive onslaught of accusations. After thirty minutes of feuding, we shut up. We had almost arrived in Philadelphia.

Philadelphia: 10 miles
We were almost to safety and out of the car when a glaring premonition began screaming at me. I was feeling the accumulation of two years of endless torture, despair, and hopelessness.

Philadelphia: 5 miles
I couldn't fucking take it anymore. I hated what my life had become. I needed to take action.

Philadelphia: 2 miles
"We can't keep living this way, Lauren," I said, rupturing her anger.

Philadelphia: Next exit
"I'm sorry, Lauren; this has to end."

Parked at a random street corner in downtown Philly:
"I can't do any of this any longer."

"You're making a mistake, Spencer. Don't do this," replied Lauren. "You owe this to yourself and to me to see this through, for better or worse." Her plea fell on deaf ears as I started to see the light at the end of the tunnel. "Please, Spence, what are you doing? You're going to regret this!"

I hailed a taxi for her.

"So it's true. It's really over. This is really happening," she said.

I replied with a raw and authentic certainty that I had not felt in ages. It felt fucking amazing.

"Yes, Lauren, it's over."

With a look of despair on her face, she handed back my great-grandmother's ring and got into the cab.

I turned around and walked away. Jeff was waiting nearby.

"It's over, dude."

Jeff knew exactly what I meant.

He knew that I had finally summoned up the courage to make the long-overdue decision to end the engagement and relationship with Lauren. The relief was overwhelming. The train arrived at the station, and I was home free. Jeff gave me a long embrace and took me straight to a nearby Scottish pub to get me talking—and drinking, of course.

I had no idea where Lauren went that day, and I didn't care. Everything about us clicked off. I hadn't gone on a binge for a couple of weeks. The timing was perfect. I was ready to get hammered and to be honest. No one knew or understood what I had experienced with Lauren. No one! My friends were basing what they knew on hearsay from other friends. It seemed I had left everyone in the dark, not only about Lauren but about everything. Jeff and I sat at that bar for hours.

After I had come clean about everything, Jeff started to talk. He told me that *all* of my friends started sharing their opinions about me without including me. Over the next several months, more and more would be revealed about what they had said. And that affected me—a lot.

Here's a brief summary of what ultimately came out:

Jeff, Matt, Matt, Brian, Hillary, and basically everyone with whom I'd been especially tight over the years had loosely planned to boycott Lauren's and my wedding. No one in my life could make sense of what was happening in our relationship. Jeff had expressed the most concern before I proposed to her, but I didn't listen. So had Matt Molyneux. His frustration pertained to her mindless aspirations to open a hair salon in a strip mall in suburban Philadelphia, which, by the way, I was going to fund. Matt's sentiments were now starting to make sense.

It turns out that the majority of my friends, from all walks of life, couldn't stand Lauren. Even to this day, when Lauren's name comes up, Jeff swears that he would have tried to hit her with his car. One of Jeff's ex-girlfriends, with whom Lauren had had a casual friendship, told him that Lauren lied to me about being on birth control for the last year of our relationship. Therefore, it was no surprise that she became pregnant. Many of my friends understood that this was a means for her to hook me once and for all. Having a child with Lauren would have done just that.

Furthermore, Vanessa's asking the private investigator to look into the suspicious e-mails had, in fact, nothing to do with me. It turns out that Vanessa and her PI discovered that through fake e-mail accounts, *Lauren* was sending the vicious e-mails to Vanessa. The PI had traced the IP addresses to several computers that Lauren used, including her school computer from her job at a private high school in Baltimore. Even after I had departed from Bend, Lauren continued the onslaught of online attacks. Perhaps in a momentary lapse of reason, Lauren even sent Vanessa a scathing e-mail from one of *my* e-mail accounts.

Later on, after Vanessa and I had renewed our friendship, she shared with me some of what Lauren had written to her. I couldn't believe my eyes when I read how Lauren was attacking her with absolutely asinine and unbelievable shit. The content of the e-mails was beyond appalling. Absolutely beyond appalling. Revolting.

After the Philly debacle, I headed home to Massachusetts to regroup and figure out what the hell I was going to do. It was fortunate that Matt Molyneux was out of school and had some free time to commiserate with me. I headed to Boston and drank everything in his house from sunrise to sundown over three painful days.

After consuming the liquor that I could afford, apart from Matt's stash, I concluded that I would move back to Bend. I figured out that Bend would be the best place to reestablish myself and start over. However, there was one problem. Everything I owned, what little I had, was still in Baltimore at the apartment where Lauren and I were living.

Of most importance was the ring my great-grandfather had left me. As the secretary of the Treasury in the Truman administration, he was given a solid gold ring engraved with the seal of the Treasury, and I had inherited it. The ring was priceless to me, and Lauren knew it. I was in a panic that she would hold it hostage until we talked.

Since I was shacking up with Matt, I recruited him to come with me to Baltimore to reclaim my possessions. Without hesitation, he was ready to go. Matt was always down for a great adventure. This was going to be a pure Gong Show for him to witness. For payment, I told him that I would give him my TV from the apartment, once we were free and clear. The problem was that I wanted to make the pickup without seeing Lauren. With that challenge, we developed a scheme to do the job quickly and undetected.

I contacted Heather, my friend who—ironically—had initially introduced me to Lauren, to see if she could find out where Lauren was. After doing some digging, Heather found out that she was at her parents' home in Pennsylvania for an undetermined amount of time. Within ten minutes of receiving the information, Matt and I jumped into my car and headed to Baltimore for the grab.

Not three hours later, I got a call from Heather. "Abort, abort! Lauren went back to Baltimore!" Fuck. We immediately turned around and headed back to Boston to regroup.

After another day of intense drinking, we made the decision to try again. This time, however, we knew Lauren would be in town. God, how I wanted to get on with my life! Before our second attempt, Matt contacted Lauren and gave her some simple terms to abide by once we reached town. He became all lawyer-like; it was fucking awesome. The deal was that I would be at the apartment at 8:00 a.m. and out in an hour. She agreed that she would not be there.

The next morning, Matt and I woke up and made our way over to the apartment to get the retrieval process going. Once we arrived, however, Lauren showed up—to no one's surprise—with her friend Dana. Matt stood between us and said that Lauren would have two minutes to talk, and then she'd have to go. Matt and Dana exited the apartment. The mood was solemn, and the air was thick. Lauren stated her final plea and finished by repeating that I was making a huge mistake. In response, I shook my head and stayed silent. Once her time was up, Matt came back in to continue our task. On her way out, Lauren turned around and presented me with my great-grandfather's ring. After handing me the ring, she exited for good. I'd never see her again.

Once she was out of the way, Matt and I frantically packed every possession I could claim as mine into every nook and cranny of my 4-Runner. After filling my car to the brim, we began driving, and Matt said, "Wait! We forgot something." He quickly ran back into the apartment for the last time. A few seconds later, he came out with my TV on his back, the cords dangling everywhere and dragging along the driveway. Matt was convinced that it had to come with us. He was completely against Lauren watching my TV for any longer. With time running out and Lauren's imminent return on the horizon, we literally shoved the TV into the car without regard for any of the car's contents. Somehow the fucking thing fit. Matt's day had been made.

CHAPTER 14

Check out Gareth Emery's podcast, episode 268. About halfway through the episode, Gareth, a British electronic dance music (EDM) producer, does his weekly e-mail shout-outs. My buddy Kieran had sent in an e-mail to the show, days before I was scheduled to race in the 2014 North Face 50 Miler. The e-mail asked if Gareth could wish me good luck at the race, explaining that every time I trained, I had a Gareth set blaring into my earbuds. Gareth ended up reading the e-mail on #268. It was fucking awesome.

Sophomore year at St. Lawrence, Kieran was playing some weird shit on his stereo in his suite one day. It was a mixture of heavy beats and a new-age synthesizer sound. I didn't know what to make of it at first because the only music that interested me was played by bands like White Lion, Faster Pussycat, Cinderella, and, of course, Mötley Crüe. Curious enough to hear more, I asked him to burn me a CD featuring some DJ named Ayla. The sounds and melodies of trance/EDM instantly captivated me.

In 2000, the trance/progressive music scene was firmly on my radar. Paul Oakenfold had recently released "Tranceport," Moby was finishing up his breakout record "Play," and Underworld was riding high from its hit single "Born Slippy" from the *Trainspotting* soundtrack. Trance music had not hit the mainstream yet, but Kieran seemed to be on top of it. With his help, my new music obsession was born.

Fall 2007

One advantage to living in Baltimore was its proximity to New York City. Armin van Buuren, one of the world's most famous trance DJs, was on his way to town, and Kieran had picked up a handful of tickets for a bunch of our friends who lived in the city. Seeing Armin would only be my second trance/progressive show, the first being Paul Oakenfold the previous summer in Portland with Lauren and Jeff. I was fucking stoked to see Armin; he was the king of the scene at the time. The show was likely to be an insane experience.

On the noon train to New York on the day of the show, the excitement for the evening's impending madness overcame me. I was also going to escape Lauren for the day, so I decided to treat myself with a dozen or so Coors Lights within two hours of boarding the train. If I was going to a trance show that night, then I'd have to act like a raver, whatever that really meant. I wanted to blow my fucking mind.

When I arrived at Kieran's apartment, no one noticed my drunken stupor because everyone else was already hammered. Happy that no one noticed my state of inebriation, I continued to drink full steam. The NYC boys and I immediately dove into copious amounts of vodka.

The show was at NYC's legendary Pacha nightclub. Fortunately, Kieran had secured a VIP table for us at the club so that we could have our own little corner to ourselves. By the time Armin came on at around 1:00 a.m., I had been drinking for twelve straight hours. This was going to be an amazing night: the most well-known DJ in the world along with my boys and endless amounts of vodka. What could go wrong? Besides everything?

Armin opened the show with John O'Callaghan's smash hit "Big Sky," and the floor turned into a freaking mosh pit. Everybody, including me, was going nuts. Not five minutes later, my head started to spin. I had not eaten all day; the only calories I'd consumed were from the booze. I needed something else to help me push through. So, rather than seek out some food, I convinced so random dude in the bathroom to cough up some of his coke. Score!

The next thing I remember is violently throwing up into a shiny silver champagne ice bucket with some big-ass bouncer screaming at me to get the fuck out of the club. "Dude, can't you see I'm dying!? Leave me alone!" That might have worked at a bar in Bend, but this was New York City, and I was out of my league. Within seconds, I was shown the door and cast into the New York City streets by myself. It was 3:00 a.m. Four hours later, I found myself stirring on a couch in Kieran's apartment with no idea how I got there. I was proud of myself that I had taken on New York and had won. Then my phone rang. It was Lauren. I was supposed to meet her at 10:00 a.m. back in Philadelphia so that we could catch a Flyers hockey game. Oh, fuck, I thought, this is going to be tricky. Kieran had some vodka in his kitchen, so rather than go for a morning coffee to attempt to come back to life, I put the bottle to my lips and chugged for what seemed like a minute. Seconds later I was in the bathroom, vomiting up everything that was left in my stomach.

Miraculously, I found my way to Grand Central to catch the train to Philly. I felt like absolute hell. A mini-blackout wiped out my memory of the train ride. I must have smelled like a sewer drain to the rest of the passengers. When Lauren met me at the train station, she immediately caught on to what was happening and began to accuse me endlessly about how she could not trust me. The fight carried on for hours, exacerbated by my terrible hangover. Between my trips to the bathroom in our hotel room to puke, Lauren kept raging; I had never seen her this way. Announcing that she was going to dinner by herself, she looked at me in my pathetic state and handed me her engagement ring. "You can give this back to me when you grow up," she said. It was the second time since getting engaged that she had given the ring back to me. With that, she walked out the door. I went to the bathroom to throw up again.

CHAPTER 15

January 2008

With my Toyota 4-Runner loaded down, filled with everything that remained from the last couple of years, I tore out of Massachusetts and began the trip across the country to Bend. Going back to Oregon was the right choice. Despite my mistakes, I still managed to make several close friends and develop good relationships during my five-year residence in central Oregon before relocating to Baltimore. It was from those friends that I would seek support in the rebuilding process after the shit-show I went through with Lauren.

Locked and loaded with No-Doz energy pills, a log of Grizzly Wintergreen, and a new CD that Dan and Kieran had mixed, I reached and passed through Chicago from Massachusetts in only a day. I must have broken the speed limit for twenty straight hours.

Right around Des Moines, Iowa, I called Davis:

"Hey, dude, Lauren and I split. I'm coming home," I said.

Davis simply replied, "I've been waiting for this call for a while. We're here for you."

He and his wife, Lisa, with whom I'd also become close, weren't surprised one iota that the relationship with Lauren had exploded. They agreed with the rest of my friends that it was a disaster waiting to happen.

The second phone call during my road trip was to my friends Bill (with whom I had formed the road-cycling team) and Brenna:

"Hey, dude, I'm coming home. Can I sleep on your futon?"

Bill's response was, "As long as it means you're back in Bend."

The third call went to one of my former mentors at the Inn of the Seventh Mountain, Anne McDonald. She had broken off from the hospitality industry to start her own recruiting company. I explained the situation, and she promised that she would try to help find me a job.

Over the four-day drive, I did everything I could think of to pave the way to a relatively smooth transition into a reasonable life. The minute I arrived in Bend, I went straight to Anne's office. She had mentioned that she might have a job lead for me, so I wanted to jump on it as soon as possible. Forty-five minutes later, after chatting with her, she offered me a job as her partner to help build her new business. I was shocked. I accepted.

Somehow I had also been able to keep my house. While in Baltimore, I had found a renter to help offset some of the exorbitant monthly 100 percent interest-only mortgage loan that was sucking me dry every month. A week after coming back to Bend, I had the tenant kicked out so that I could move into the house that Lauren and I once shared. All I had to my name in my two-thousand-square-foot house was a lawn chair, my TV that Matt had insisted on retrieving (he felt bad for me, so he let me keep it), and an air mattress. Strewn across the kitchen were a couple of spoons, a fork, and a single dish that I had picked up at Goodwill. Even though I was grateful to have escaped Maryland, I was alone in my home, feeling sorry for myself.

Being in that house was a constant reminder of the dreams that died and the future that never was.

My situation began to slowly improve. Although I was still mourning from the trauma that I had experienced with Lauren, I was able to uncover some incentive for turning my life around. The first big step, other than finding a job, was to get back on the bike. I was clearly out shape. Because I had fallen into Lauren's ideal image for me, "Fat Spence," I had let my body go.

By the time I reached Bend, I felt like a fat-ass. Keeping my ongoing promise to Brian, I borrowed one of Bill's road bikes and rode every single day, rain, snow, sun, or sleet. The weather didn't matter; motivation drove me more than ever to get in shape. The urgency was remarkable. I couldn't believe that I would ever go through another period of my life when I wasn't in shape. I had already tried twice before, and each time, my life unraveled due to unforeseen circumstances. My overall health depended on being fit, and I would not turn my back on it.

But alcohol was my downfall. Once the paychecks rolled in, I began to treat myself a little. Hell, I deserved it right? I had escaped a near-disaster by the skin of my teeth. This is how I justified my drinking.

My daily routine for several months went as follows: work, ride, go to McDonald's, go to 7-Eleven for some CAMO XXX, then go back home to pass out. I could handle the booze this time because I had returned to exercising. I had slipped back into the old habits that I had formed before I left Bend for Baltimore. Whatever, I thought. At least I was working and riding. That was all that mattered.

Even though I was emotionally broken after Lauren's destruction of my life, Anne introduced me one night at happy hour to one of her new friends, Hannah, a gal that had just relocated to Bend from San Francisco. At first glance, she was attractive in every way I could imagine. Smart, athletic, attractive and full of life. After being so downtrodden by the gray cloud that seemed to follow Lauren around, I was immediately drawn to Hannah's personality and adventurous tendencies. A few weeks after meeting, we began to date.

As winter turned to spring that year, my life kept moving forward. To my surprise, Anne had purchased me a brand-new road bike as a bonus for Q1 2008. I had spent the last three months beating the shit out of Bill's bike, so to have a fresh new ride was amazing. Hannah and I were forging an incredible relationship. After spending so much of my energy coping with the upheaval involving the last girl in my life, I was now thankfully less and less preoccupied with it. Hannah was really into road biking, and we quickly became riding partners as well as companions. Although we had our ups and downs that year, having her as my girlfriend helped to restore my sense of purpose.

That spring, I went back to racing. Two years before, Lauren had completely dumped on my hopes of getting back into bike racing. Well, here I was with my team, fit and racing in the Peloton again. Beginning to race made me feel better than I ever could have imagined. I had rebooted in my element, and I felt comfortable being there.

In June of 2008, the fight with the banks to keep up with my mortgage costs was a losing battle. The appraisal of my house in the summer of '06 at $335K decreased to $175K just two years later. No one would even entertain doing a refinancing for me. I had been bleeding money trying to keep that house. I had joined so many people in the harsh reality of what was happening to the world after the market crash of 2007 that it was necessary to pull it together and give my keys back to the bank. I foreclosed on the only home I'd ever owned. Once I bit the bullet and decided to follow through with the inevitable, it was liberating. I haven't regretted making that decision for one single second since.

By fall, my financial footing was becoming solid. I had my own apartment, my own furniture, a terrific girlfriend, and even a little cash to put away every month. Since more cash was in my pocket, I graduated to drinking better alcohol. The CAMO XXX 12.8 percent malt liquor transformed into fashionable and local Central Oregon microbrew IPA and a bottle of Crown Royal whiskey now and then. Bend was becoming the microbrew capital of the West Coast, so why couldn't I be a part of the culture? I turned into a self-proclaimed beer snob.

Unfortunately, I took it a little further than that. I began drinking in secret again, much like I did toward the end of the situation with Lauren and even all the way back to my senior year at St. Lawrence. When Hannah and I would have friends over for dinner at her house, I would often sneak downstairs and chug a bit of whatever bottle of liquor she had in the cabinet. I also started drinking and driving more, believing that because I was drinking good beer instead of the shit I picked up at the corner market, driving was not a problem.

As the temperature started to drop, a harbinger of winter months ahead, everything turned to shit again. I started to withdraw from Hannah, my friends, and my parents. I felt something coming on, and I couldn't explain it. I clearly remember being at Mount Bachelor attempting to ski one afternoon in order to break out of it. I couldn't move; my body felt cold and stiff. Later that afternoon, I said to Hannah that I needed some time for myself for a few days to try to figure out what was going on with me. She agreed.

To combat the depression that I was undergoing, I went straight to the 7-Eleven and bought as much alcohol as I could afford. For three days, I sat in my apartment and drank by myself, having cut off all communication from the outside world. A second trip to Sageview Psychiatric Center was slowly appearing on the horizon.

Journal Entries

December 29, 2008

4:30 a.m.—Squirming in bed, half-drunk from a three-day binge on CAMO XXX malt liquors. Can't sleep, this is the lowest I've ever been. Call Dad, call Mom, call Hannah. Heading to the ER and back to Sageview. I cannot deal with this on my own any longer.

6:30 a.m.—Emergency room. Took blood, tried to sleep, nicest guy there was Bob the nurse who got me a breakfast burrito. Emergency rooms suck.

11:30 a.m.—Sageview check-in. The patients, my housemates: Ricky (cutter), Chris (bald head, ex-gang member), Chris (meth addict), Johnny (manic redhead, negotiating with parole), Candace (looked like she was pregnant), Susan (five-year-old girl stuck in the body of a fifty-five-year-old woman), Rex (old guy, won't shut up), Luke (going through a divorce, has tattoos), Sarah (psycho Asian), Bobby (quiet old woman), Tracy (sweet older lady), Jack (wears headphones and walks around laughing).

December 30, 2008

- I am an adrenaline junky, can't be mindful and enjoy the present moment. Evidence for this is cycling, skiing, Adderall, Ritalin, chewing tobacco, coffee, Red Bull, alcohol, cocaine, partying, stimulation, trance, sales, and money. I am always feeling anxious, always asking myself, What's next?
- I can't be in the moment, stay in the moment. Today, Prozac is making me feel like climbing the walls. Am I running from something with this need for adrenaline?

December 31, 2008

- Things to work on: self-confidence, personality, tendency to be an adrenaline junky, family issues, depression, my relationship with Hannah, future of my job, being in the moment, obsession with athletics, my weight, mindfulness, acceptance, fucking Lauren.
- Breathing, closing your eyes. Start with three minutes a day, and work it up to twenty.
- Men are depressed because they have a need to find the female within them, to be unselfish and giving. Why are we all at Sageview? ATTENTION. I'm here to take accountability for my life.
- Who is my shadow? What do I despise in other people: success, money, etc.? This is not criticizing other people; it's a matter of befriending your shadow. Dream and be curious. Figure out your mistaken belief about yourself and flip it. No drinking for sixty days while the meds take effect. I will know if I'm bipolar II after four to six weeks. Can I nurture myself along with being in a relationship?
- Distractions in my life include friends, work, money, my house, my boss, booze, chew, cycling, lifting, parents, radio, TV, iPod.
- I owe nothing to nobody! Save yourself! Do one thing at a time. When I eat, I eat. When I sleep, I sleep. I am #1.

January 1, 2009

- Happy fucking New Year. Fuck this shit.
- Tackling issues with my past relationship with Lauren: Why was I lied to? Why did we get engaged? Was it my fault? Why did I feel guilty and sad? Why did she do the things to me that she did? Can I ever rebound from this? Can I ever get my confidence back?

- Thinking is an ability. All of your skills don't mean anything unless you practice. I have a lack of focus; I'm always switching it up: skiing, cycling, wanting to be a DJ, marriage, real estate, money, work. I've always wanted to be on the cover of *Bend Living* (one of Bend's premier magazines). Reality is relative.
- Goals for 2009: Peace of mind (trim the adrenaline). Do things for yourself in all scopes. Work on my self-confidence. Be in the moment. Embrace mindfulness.

January 2, 2009

- Karen (nurse): If Hannah doesn't want the relationship, then there is no relationship. I have a concern with someone who does not want to be with me through and through, through the tough shit. Depression is a disease, like cancer; it doesn't go away. What do I have left here in Bend?
- Monica (nurses' aid, so freaking cute): Schedule twenty minutes a day to get pissed at the relationship you had with Lauren. Put yourself first. No one else can change your attitude. That has to come from within. Food fuels the mind. Practice spirituality, mindfulness, and meditation.

January 3, 2009

- Number-one goal is peeling back the issues, recognizing them, and figuring out how to deal with them moving forward, for myself, by myself. To cope, be mindful and accepting, breathe, relax, read, and exercise.
- Egocentrism: kids thinking that they are the root and cause of the problems for their parents, certainly a theme in my life.
- Rational mind combined with emotional mind equals a wise mind. Wise mind has a balance of thinking and feeling.
- People to talk to about teaching: Brian, Buffy, Matt.

January 4, 2009

- My critical voice: I can't be in a successful relationship. No girlfriends for me for a long time. When am I going to let Hannah know?
- Things I obsess about: Trance, cars, money, clothes, cycling, weight, fitness, music. Are all of these *my* values? Maybe? Maybe not?
- Impulse ideas for a new job: get into being a DJ to impress my NYC friends; drive around the West Coast as a journeyman and get odd jobs; teach in Spain (because my angel nurse Monica said so); go get my MSW (master's in social work—fallback plan).
- There is no need to tell everyone your plans for fear of rejection. I am a work in progress; I am making decisions for myself every day. I am worth getting to know. Was the goal for coming back to Bend from Baltimore to get back to Sageview? Oregon might not be the place for me.

January 5, 2009

- Discharge day.
- My heart is racing, I'm nervous, and I want to stay here at Sageview because it feels safe, a home. I am lonely, empty. I am a new person but won't realize it until I'm out of it. You don't know you're in a recession until you're out of it.
- You cannot drink. Not drinking is going to make this better, easier to handle.
- Just called my boy Tim to start scheduling spin times on our stationary bikes. It'll be good to have a training schedule in place. Also talked to my boy Erod, and he said, "Do what you gotta do for yourself, no one else. Keep your head up."

It took another six days at Sageview to reset my body and mind. Since it was my second time there, I was familiar with the routine, so I knew what to expect. Perhaps the biggest difference was that I was fucking ready to do some work. I understood what the doctors and therapists were saying, and I treated every single hour as though I *was* getting a master's degree, soaking up information like a sponge. It was an amazing experience, I learned more about myself in those six days than I had in the past six years. My life was returning. After I left, it took the next six months to right the ship.

Hannah and I had called it quits, in both of our best interests, but I didn't let that stop me from building myself back up. Over the next several months, my days went like this: eat, work, train, eat, write in my journal, read, sleep. Every single day, I kept that routine. And perhaps the biggest physical achievement that I endured? I didn't drink once. I had maintained sobriety for six solid months.

During this stay at Sageview, I truly began to learn what alcohol can do to a mind already deficient in serotonin production, a trait of those suffering from depression. Alcohol is a fucking depressant! Even though I understood I had a problem with alcohol, I didn't think I was an alcoholic. My pride wouldn't accept the notion of being one of "those" people who sat in dark rooms, chain-smoking cigarettes, and pounding coffee while talking about their darkest feelings and emotions.

To help in my recovery, I had reintegrated a weekly dose of psychotherapy and a rigorous, focused work schedule. And to top it all off, I started to become a player again in the road-cycling Peloton. Having lost connection with the cycling team while I was stuck in emotional and physical purgatory, I wanted to reinstate myself as our team leader. Pieces of my life were really starting to click together. Then, one night in June, I got a text from my buddy Derek. "There's someone who I think you should meet."

Derek had a friend, Laura, who was my age, smart, attractive, and single. Since getting out of Sageview, I had more or less shut down any possibility of even meeting new girls; I had neither interest nor self-confidence. But something inside me told me that I should loosen up, that maybe I was ready at least to meet someone new. My biggest challenge in attending that casual get-together was my fear of how I was going to be cool, funny, likeable, and attractive. On the drive down to the bar where we were all going to meet, I made the conscious decision that maybe one beer, to loosen up, wouldn't be such a bad thing. By drinking that first beer, along with the several others that I had that evening, all of the work that I had done for myself over the last half year disappeared in a flash. It was almost like I picked up exactly where I had left off at the end of 2008.

Starting that evening, I drank heavily, even for my standards, for the next three years. Laura, who turned out to be an amazing woman, ended up leaving Bend to return to Florida for a job. Her departure was a bummer. The way it had before, drinking gave me confidence, and I had convinced myself that confidence made me more attractive to girls. With those simple rules, I created the formula that more drinking equals more girls, which equals having more fun. And so another chapter of this life I thought I was living was about to be begin. Enter "the pile."

Just like any pile, mine started small and grew over time. With women, I created a new addiction for myself, not sexual in nature but emotional. Up to this point in my life, I had been involved with some wonderful women, excluding Lauren; I am still close with many of them. Now that drinking reenergized my confidence, I became entangled in the thrill of the chase, the ever-elusive attention, and developed an attraction to a certain type of female. I wanted to be with girls who needed my help to progress in their lives; girls I could fix and who, in turn, would wind up being the "one and only" for me. That was my formula. Girls became projects instead of people. My careless and selfish behavior lasted for many years until eventually I was forced to confront its repercussions head on.

My other addiction was road cycling. From 2009 to 2011, between drinking, I dedicated my free time to become the best cyclist I could be. It became a terrific way to fuel my ego, which in many ways had become bigger than ever. In 2010, I led my Category 3 team into the Cascade Cycling Classic stage race, a well-known Pacific Northwest biking race. As the team leader, I rallied my teammates, persuading them to believe that we could do some damage in the overall standings. Working with others fueled my ego even more.

One incident with cycling, which shows how the sport became an obsession, happened in the summer of 2011. As the team leader and director, I took my team, which was among the strongest in the state of Oregon, to race the Cascade Cycling Classic in Bend. The stakes were high this year. Since we were on our hometown course, we were going to lay everything down to get one of our guys on the podium for the overall general classification (typically a top-three result). And adding to the advantage, the team happened to be in great shape, better than I had ever seen before.

Unfortunately, by the last kilometer of the first stage, I had laid a little too much on the line. I crossed the finish line in a hyponatremic (overhydration) state and wound up in the medical tent, convulsing and hyperventilating in front of my mother, for heaven's sake, who had come to Oregon to see me participate in a bike race for the first time. While I was in the medical tent, about to be hooked up to an IV, Mike Larsen, my coach, came in and told the medics to stop immediately; he knew I wasn't dehydrated, like the doctors thought. If it weren't for Mike looking out for me, the situation would've grown worse. Overall, my ego took a massive hit. My love for cycling took the other hit.

After spending a few days recovering physically from the incident, along with plenty of binge drinking to drown my sorrows, I all but quit the sport. I had burned out. I thought that I deserved more, and when I didn't get it, after working so hard to become a good cyclist, I took the easy way out and let pride get the best of me. Another multimonth bender to cure the most recent hit to my self-confidence took place. In this period of time, I got mixed up in a pretty toxic crowd, hanging with drug dealers, pill pushers, and would-be alcoholics.

That fall, the innocence and purity of Bend, or what was left of it for me, completely disappeared. At one time, Bend was my playground, my identity, and the place where I became an adult. After having gone through two visits to a psychiatric hospital, a suicide attempt, pure hell with Lauren, and a development of a dependency to alcohol, the town of Bend could give me nothing more. By December 2011, I had to call it quits with the town for which I had once had the deepest love affair. Fueled with those heavy sentiments, I ran away—not far, but far enough so that I could escape some of my demons. Enter Corvallis, Oregon, for which I had great affection, mostly because of the memories that lay there.

CHAPTER 16

January 2012

Her name was Kristin, and she was fucking gorgeous. She worked at a coffee shop just a block away from my office on Century Drive in Bend. During the summer of 2011, I was working as a development officer at the local homeless teen shelter. I would make an excuse to get coffee three times a day if I knew she was working. Eventually I knew her schedule and would even go in a fourth time to get some iced water, which was also readily available at the office.

Kristin seemed sweet, funny, and vivacious. She was small in the perfect way: fit, blond, and with a face one could only imagine. Kristin was the most beautiful girl I had ever laid eyes on. Yes, it was love at first sight. In the middle of my destructive final months in Bend, I had managed to create a friendship with Kristin, mostly by flirting with her at her coffee stand. One night, we happened to run into each other at Bend's Astro Lounge and had one of those naïve, inebriated yet intriguing conversations about how bad an idea it was that we were in the same place at the same time. I had already snorted up a heavy dose of Adderall that evening, so my feelings were even more heightened by the rush of amphetamines that permeated my body. Seeing her out of her work mode, at a time when her infectious candor bloomed, the innocent love I had for her grew even deeper. Nothing had happened sexually between us because she was in the middle of a divorce. How the fuck was I going to make this relationship happen?

At the time that Derek's text (yes, that same Derek) came in, I had already run away from Bend to Corvallis. Derek suggested that there was someone he thought that I should spend more time with: fucking Derek, you have such shitty timing. He mentioned that I was acquainted with her and, according to him, she may be interested in spending some time getting to know me better. After he strung me along for a while, Derek told me that the girl he was talking about was Kristin—yup, my coffee-stand angel, Kristin. I had no idea that he and Kristin even knew each other. All I said in response was, "Fuck you, don't fuck with me." The joke was on me because Derek had been telling me the truth about Kristin.

Kristin relocated to Portland to go to school. Once Derek coughed up her number, I immediately reached out to see if she wanted to grab dinner. I was not going to wait; I had to see her. After both of us had moved away from Bend, we fell out of touch, and I didn't have the balls to get her number when I had the chance in Bend. She agreed to have dinner with me, and not one week later, I found myself sitting in a low-lit restaurant with Kristin, sharing cocktails, laughs, and stories. I couldn't fucking believe this was happening. I must've pinched myself in the ass a dozen times that night. At the end of the evening, standing outside of the restaurant, Kristin asked me if I wanted to come with her and a group of her friends to a Miike (there are two i's) Snow concert later the following month. "Yup!" Done deal.

As she walked away to go to her car, I stood there, speechless, wondering how this was happening to me. Maybe fantasy shit like this does actually happen to people? It was self-doubt talking then, because when I reached Corvallis, I was dealing with the effects of a four-month hangover from excessive amounts of speed and booze. Yes, I played it cool enough back in Bend to catch her eye, but I was still convinced that there was no way someone as great as Kristin would end up in my life. No fucking way.

Fortunately, Kristin didn't see my weaknesses. She saw something else. After her divorce was finalized, we met up to go catch the show we had planned to attend together. I did my very best to get my head out of my ass to feel worthy of being around her. I put on my best pair of jeans and a slick shirt and tried to look as cool as ever. We ended up spending the night together, and I thought that I actually had a chance to date Kristin.

Come springtime, Kristin and I continued to meet. When we weren't physically around each other, we'd always flirt in an exchange of text messages. Our relationship was relatively innocent, much like one I might have had in junior high. We held hands, made out in random parks while walking her dog, and thoroughly enjoyed each other's company. I was constantly giddy around her. Maybe I had struck it rich and found the one? I wanted it to be the case so badly that it hurt.

Journal Entry

Don't fuck it up with Kristin like you did with Sarah. Be her friend, with no expectations; be honest, you have nothing to lose. This doesn't have to be fueled by drugs and alcohol. She's innocent! You weren't 100 percent honest with Sarah; half of the thrill was about the rush of doing cocaine with her. God, how sexy was that? Even though you get reassurance from her that you're attractive and likeable, treat it differently than you did with Sarah. This doesn't have to be fueled on lies. She's easily the hottest girl you've ever been with, dude, and she's fucking rad! Does it get any better than this? Maybe things are turning around, maybe I deserve this, and maybe I've found the one!

Then she decided to introduce me to her parents in her hometown of Roseburg. Perhaps this was her way of putting me through the next litmus test in the relationship. Hell, the more people I could charm in her life the better. I wanted her family to support our being together.

After having a fun day meeting her family, riding four-wheelers, and lying in the sun, I thought that what was coalescing between us might be really special. I also began to feel whole, healed, like I was being "me" again. After having dinner and kissing good-bye, I departed, as happy as ever. That would be the last time I'd ever see Kristin again.

A few days later, I received a surprising e-mail that said, in summary, that she just didn't believe that we would make a good couple. I was devastated. She was that special woman! I went from feeling on top of the fucking world to feeling as small as a cockroach. I hated it. So instead of dealing with it responsibly, I began another month-long binge by myself, in isolation. The self-worth that I had built, the wholeness, the peace of mind, sailed straight out the fucking window one more time.

CHAPTER 17

One Saturday night in Bend in the fall of 2011, I sat in my unlit living room alone, waiting for Jeff to get off of work so that we could run around downtown looking for trouble. On my coffee table sat a big-old twenty-two-ounce Ninkasi IPA along with a plate covered with chopped-up Adderall, which I had stolen from a friend earlier in the week. It was 8:00 p.m., and I had another hour to burn before Jeff was off for the night. This was pathetic; I knew it in my core.

My discontent with Bend was at an all-time high. My loneliness triggered raising the ante to ingest prescription drugs as well as cocaine. Based on the scene that was unfolding in my living room that evening, I knew that a change was inevitable; I just didn't know what. So, as tears streamed down my face, I rolled up a dollar bill, snorted the remainder of the Adderall, chugged the remaining IPA, and headed downtown to find Jeff.

My addictions had taken over. Bend had become a dark place that I needed to leave. Instead of living in Bend to be a part of the endurance community, as had been my intent way back in 1998, I had resorted to chasing cocaine dealers around town late at night. The aura, magic, and mystique of calling Bend my home had completely diminished. In a state of utter unhappiness in December of 2011, I ran away to Corvallis, Oregon.

In a twist of fate, Davis had relocated his family to Corvallis so that he could be the general manager at the biggest hotel in the area a few months earlier. Fortunately, he needed of a director of sales. I was able to jump on board at the hotel where he was working.

On paper, the transition was seamless. I had a place to live, a bike, a car, the Smiths, and a little bit of money to get started. I hadn't been in a better place financially since my days of Lauren and selling real estate. With a little more money-handling experience under my belt, I arrived in Corvallis on a mission to avoid repeating the habitually stupid financial mistakes of the past. The move to Corvallis reignited my life; this was a place where I could begin a sustainable existence, not only with work but also with my entire lifestyle. Unfortunately, I was so hell-bent on rebooting that I forgot to look around my new town more closely.

Within weeks of moving to Corvallis, I was already trying to figure out a way back to Bend. I hated living in Corvallis at first. But I was able to push through some of the disdain that was growing around it. Being busy with the transition at work, I was able to ignore the gut feeling of having made a mistake.

Corvallis is the home of Oregon State University, one of the biggest agricultural institutions in the United States. My first task in coming to town, work-wise, was to improve the relationship that our hotel had with the University. The previous management had totally fucked up the connection from a business standpoint, and I was the guy enlisted, along with Davis, to help mend the wounds. This meant that I worked directly with OSU athletics, my beloved Beavers, tending to their hospitality needs throughout their respective seasons and making sure that everyone was happy. In many ways, my job was pretty great because I spent most of that first season working hand in hand with several of the athletic administrators, coaches, and recruits when they rolled through town on their respective recruiting trips. During that year, I had an exclusive access to the Beavers that most people never had a chance to experience.

I also took it upon myself to clean up my act a bit with the drinking. I had had a pretty wild time leading up to the move, so I wanted to dry out and reacquire some fitness that I had lost since quitting cycling just a few months earlier. As time wore on, Corvallis became not so bad.

The interesting part about Bend was that the town was littered with physical memories—such as the dive bars and other places—that I only related to alcohol. In Corvallis, other than during football game days, I really didn't have the visual cues of places where I had really fucked up. Yeah, there are lots of bars in Corvallis, but I didn't associate any memories with them.

Journal Entry

Is my future in Corvallis? I'm six months into this experiment, and I need to give myself six more months to make a decision to stay longer. I want to give this town a fair shot. I only had four beers all week last week. Not drinking makes me sharper. The twenty-minute beer buzz I get after pounding a double IPA goes away really quickly, it's boring, and once the first one is down the hatch, I'm unproductive for the rest of the night. Fuck booze. Things I like about Corvallis include the foliage, the sound of rain, and the trails. They're fucking gorgeous to run on!

Maybe the goal of coming to Corvallis is to be comfortable in being alone. Perhaps give it a solid year to work on myself before deciding what to do next. Yes, I'm bored, but I'm living a healthy lifestyle. I wish I had MOVED TO Corvallis rather than RUN AWAY from Bend. Fuck it, I'm just going to spend my time here getting fit as hell. It's the perfect little town to train in and achieve levels of fitness that I've never experienced.

Athletically, I also became aware of another sport. Brian had approached me to see if I wanted to team up with him to do some ridiculous and absurd race in Colorado called the TransRockies Run, a six-day trail-running stage race covering 120 miles and twenty thousand feet of elevation gain. Still burned out on cycling, I agreed to attempt the challenge with him. This sport that I was going to try had a name: ultra-running. The sport of ultra-running involves running insanely long distances in the woods. That is it.

Running has always been a challenge for me. I ran cross-country in high school at Gateway and Burke Mountain Academy, but I was usually the slowest guy on the team, mediocre at best. As a skier, I ran during the summer months to keep in shape, but again, it was something that I didn't really enjoy. My teammates always outran me.

At St. Lawrence, the trend continued. My buddy Eric and I were consistently in the back of the pack when our team would go out for training runs. Needless to say, I never once in my life thought of myself as a decent runner. In order to prepare for TransRockies, I gave my old cycling coach a call to see if he could help me out. He immediately jumped at the chance to coach me.

Blog post:
The Power of Mentors: Michael Larsen

> Around 2008, I had been competing in the Oregon Category 3 field at a fairly mediocre level. I trained a ton, always eager to work on my tan lines so that I could "fit in" with the emerging cycling community in Bend. Literally, I used to judge my fitness on the strength of my tan lines; looking back, it was ridiculous, but it was the truth nonetheless. Always eager to race, to feel a part of something, I would join my team to compete in big Oregon stage races like the Elkhorn Cycling Classic and the Cascade Cycling Classic.

*Together with Mike (left) at my two year, twelve hour,
sobriety birthday run, 2016*

However, even with all of the training and racing, I still wasn't too competitive, either physically or mentally. The cycling scene in Bend around that time was getting very intense. Local riders would all meet every Tuesday at Sunnyside Sports for the Tuesday Evening Hammerfest. This became known as the weekly Bend Cycling Championships of the World. We cared about sanctioned races; it was all about Tuesday evenings, for bragging rights. I was hooked.

One night, a dude rolled up next to me with ultra-tan legs, veins sticking out, sweat bands on, super intense. Something about him impressed me immediately: he was confident, fit, and aggressive, with testosterone coming out of his ears. I wanted what he had.

His name was Michael, the brother of the legendary Steve Larsen, another elite Bend endurance athlete. Word had it that Mike was coaching a couple of athletes in town (not that I could afford it at the time). I reached out to him to try to tap into some of his demeanor. His approach to athletics was something that I wanted to latch on to, because clearly if I was going to be a part of the uber-competitive Bend bike scene, I had to step up my game. I became addicted to getting faster.

Now, as I look back, I am coming to find out how important Mike was, and still is, in my life. He taught me not only how to train again but also to believe in myself. See, I had the physical talent, but I lacked the confidence. I was a mental shit-show, always questioning how good at cycling I was, if I fit in, how fast I appeared, how worthy I felt. Mike's approach to training was to get out of your head, give it everything you have and then some, and keep the big picture in mind. Sure, wattage was fine, hills were hard, and time trialing was tough, but unless you have the ability to believe in yourself and rise to the occasion, what's the point?

Mike pushed me and showed me how to achieve new levels of pain, to survive, and then to thrive. We would do weekly hill-climb sessions on Awbrey Butte, to the Towers; he'd ride with me, yelling in my ear, "Don't fucking slow down! Don't let up, you puss! Quit being a fucking puss." To some in town, this might come off as offensive, but I soaked it up and responded. If I was averaging 320 watts up a long climb, he'd yell and motivate me to push it to 330 watts...there is always more in the tank, sack up, get it! I had the fitness; I just needed to find the confidence to put it all together, and his methodology worked for me.

There was something about his infectious, outlandish, aggressive personality that I bought into 100 percent. With that, I became a better, more confident athlete. This past March I joined a Bend contingent in Sedona, Arizona, for a week-long bike camp. Mike was included in the bunch. It was the first time that I had left Corvallis since deciding to be sober the month before on February 11, 2014.

Going into that trip, I had a ton of anxiety and was still in the midst of sorting out a lot of the bullshit in my head. A few days beforehand, Mike sent me a text reminding me that Strava didn't matter, wattage didn't matter, elevation gain didn't matter...what mattered was the camaraderie of good friends and having fun. It's exactly what I needed to hear at the time. That week helped me to push past the pink cloud of getting sober and refocus on rediscovering the athlete I had dedicated myself to being back when I was on top of my cycling game in 2011. Having him there helped motivate me to quit being a pussy and get back to my roots once again, to rededicate myself to kicking ass.

When sobriety gets hard, I try to pull a chapter from my book of Larsenisms: sack up and get back on track. He doesn't necessarily know it, but he helps me stay sober in his own unique way.

Years ago, Mike gave me a set of tweezers to carry with me for when I was getting soft and needing some motivation to pull my head out of my ass. Those tweezers come with me everywhere I go, and that will continue. Mike will always be an important person in my life, not just as a mentor but also as a friend and training partner. If I ever get the itch to get fast on a bike again, he'll be the first person I call. Thank you, Mike, for everything. Let's run soon.

To begin with, Mike and I laid out a training plan that would pave the road for me to complete TransRockies with Brian. The first step in the process was the Eugene Marathon. During the previous two falls, I had managed to put together some decent training despite the chaos that I was creating for myself in my partying life.

For my first marathon, the California International Marathon (CIM), I threw down a Boston qualifying time of 3:08. The following year, for my second marathon, I put down a 3:05 despite being fifteen to twenty pounds over my race weight, mostly due to the copious amounts of whiskey that I had imbibed during the lead up to the race. With those two races under my belt, I was curious to see what would happen at Eugene, knowing that running had taken over my focus from road cycling. I ended up running a solid time of 3:03, my third Boston-qualifying time in as many races.

It seemed as though my body was responding to the uptick in running volume. Perhaps my cycling fitness was being transferred. I figured running Eugene as fast as I did would set me up for success leading into TransRockies.

Two weeks later, Mike and I decided that it might be a good idea to enter my first 50K. We both thought that I was fit enough to at least nail down a top ten, given what I had just done at Eugene. I chose my first ultra-marathon (defined as any race longer than the 26.2 marathon distance) in my own backyard. It was called the McDonald Forest 50K, located just north of Corvallis. Typically, a winning time for a hard 50K is in the low four-hour range. On that day I strolled, or rather crawled, into the finish area with a time of 6:15, a full hour and a half behind the top ten.

At that stage in my athletic career, that race was the hardest and most humbling event I had ever done. Even though it was a fucking difficult race, the idea of being an ultra-marathoner stuck.

After a three-week recovery from the Mac 50K, I began to spend more time on the endless trails that the McDonald Forest had to offer to better prepare for TransRockies. The race experience grounded me. I felt motivated to explore this new area; mystery and awe existed for me in those woods. Running and exploring the ground that I had survived running on a few weeks prior, I was embraced by something that was more powerful than me. I had been intimidated by this place, by this sport, and by the mental challenge of accomplishing the running of thirty miles in the hilly woods. Yet the true grandeur of the forest penetrated my soul. I was ready to better myself in this relentless ultra-endurance sport.

I was healthy and treating my body well, and I was excited to keep forging ahead with logging big miles on the trails. With this new enthusiasm, I was able to put drinking aside. Until, that is, I found myself in a dive bar in Ashland, pounding whiskey and beers right after completing my second 50K trail race.

Meanwhile, the other addictions still persisted in my life. Once again, enter "the pile."

Journal Entry

July 17, 2012

The pile and its status:

- Sarah—has a boyfriend
- Lisa—emotionally not available
- Kristin—divorced and unavailable
- Ashley—engaged
- Jenny—the "I fucked that one up" pile
- Hannah—engaged
- Lauren—gets her own fucking pile for being awful
- Nora—turned lesbian
- Sally—married

See prior list. When I started my last journal, it was during my second stint at Sageview. I was trying hard to get over Lauren. Hannah was still in the picture. By the end of that journal, I had realized what was brought on by Hannah's recent engagement. In total, 75 percent of my last journal had to do with all the girls in my life and how they affected my confidence, my ego, and my sanity. I lost sight of keeping track of my own good. I kept getting emotionally wrapped up in girls who were not available. This drove me nuts and made me question who I was several times since the journal had been started. It is time to shut the door on all of these girls, move the fuck on, and start taking care of yourself.

Where you are as of today: 167 pounds, two weeks out from TransRockies, fit as fuck, wondering who I should be with, if anyone, and bored as fuck in Corvallis, apart from the trails.

I'm starting to believe that I need a partner in life who does what I do, doesn't party a ton, is active, doesn't do coke, and lives a lifestyle that I can relate to. All of the girls in the pile took something from you, attention, and gave you nothing in return. That hurt you! Quit looking so hard, and focus on yourself during a time when you're on your own in Corvallis, without distractions. That is why you're here—to get fit, ripped, and mentally sound for the next stage in life.

"The pile" began to exemplify many of the bad decisions I had made in my life: the drinking, the drugs, the parties, the depravity, the need for attention, and the need to feel loved.

The journal entry above was written after two weeks of not drinking. During those two weeks, I began to feel good, think clearly, and process some of the shit I went through to find the root of those transgressions. The common denominator was the group of girls who I surrounded myself with—the pile—and I needed to fix it.

A couple of weeks after I wrote that journal entry, a friend of mine in Corvallis decided that he might have to address his problems with alcohol. He had been on a pretty heavy drinking streak over the past few years and wanted to determine if he was actually an alcoholic. I agreed to support him at a recovery meeting so that he didn't feel like he was on his own. Supporting a friend turned into another direction.

Ten minutes of the meeting passed. I started to get that *I* may be an alcoholic. After being introduced to what alcoholism really is, I vowed to get clean, for my own sake. I was lucky enough to show up in Colorado with a tremendous level of fitness for TransRockies, four weeks into not drinking. Even after injuring myself halfway through the race and being devastated in the process, I resisted the temptation to drink to alleviate the emotional pain of it. That was a completely atypical and welcome response.

After coming home to Corvallis post-TransRockies, I even went to a couple of early-season football games completely sober and had a blast. The more time I didn't drink, the better I felt. It was amazing. I began training again, having just recovered from TransRockies and my injury, to log miles that fall that I'd never been able to do before. My first hundred-mile running week that fall motivated me. My confidence was building, and my spirits were lifted; I couldn't have been any more prepared to keep the momentum going. Not drinking felt fucking awesome. Oh my god, I could really get used to this! I was getting lighter, leaner, and more in shape than ever. I was kicking ass.

Together with Brian (left) at the 2012 TransRockiesRun

Then, without hesitation, I let Lisa back into my life. A downward spiral was about to ensue.

CHAPTER 18

"You're hooking up with Mason? Are you fucking kidding me? That dude better have a dick the size of Canada to make up for how short he is." I hated that dude.

Chelsea had entered the stream of things. A flirty friendship between two giddy, single people had turned into—for me, at least—a full-on love affair. Like Kristin, Sarah, and Lisa, Chelsea was a picture of perfection in my eyes: attractive, fun, tall, and vibrant. Within just a few times of hanging out, I became a love-drunk puppy dog around her. Younger than me, Chelsea seemed to have what I wanted in someone. I was immediately hooked by her allure and strong character. I always wanted to know more about her; she seemed to keep her cards hidden. I couldn't understand it, and I wanted to be let in.

As we first got to know each other, we shared some good times. It was casual, silly, and playful. We would sip cocktails in her apartment, sharing life stories. We'd flick shit at each other, picking at each other innocently. None of our friends knew anything about our blossoming friendship. It seemed like we were keeping some big secret.

When Chelsea and I were on the verge of forming a solid bond, merely as friends at this point, this cocky-ass troll entered the picture and totally fucked everything up. Mason was literally five feet tall. Somehow he had been talking his way into Chelsea's life, much to my surprise.

It irked me to watch Chelsea be into other guys and talk about them. Mason was continually the subject of the conversation; all I wanted was to figure out what the fuck she saw in him. The combination of Chelsea and Mason kept me up so many nights; the anxiety of knowing they were together was unbearable. I'd never had a girl, except for Lauren, affect me so much. I was debilitated.

Journal Entry

September 25, 2013

So I've had five beers and four glasses of wine since happy hour when I heard that Mason and Chelsea were, in fact, hooking up. I also heard that Chelsea had two other dudes on the line, so I called her out on it, to which she responded by calling me and saying that we were never a thing and that what she does is not my fucking business. Fine, maybe it isn't, but at least I care! More than that ass-clown Mason. Now we're going back and forth on text, and I know it's only going to end badly.

Since the Siskiyou Out and Back 50K, I've been on a tear with partying. I'm obsessed with the fact that Chelsea may be hooking up with other dudes, like that troll Mason. Therefore, it's hurting my ego. Whatever happened to just being the cool guy and letting things play out? One of my biggest life problems is finding balance among women, training, drinking, and life.

The anxiety that Chelsea instigated seemed to equal the accumulation of all the feelings I'd ever had for a woman. I thought that I was in love with her. I knew in my heart that there was something special about our relationship. I was ready for this, ready to be in a committed relationship with someone. I wanted her to finally tell me that I was the one for her, that she was ready, and that she felt the same way. I waited and waited for her to admit that she was in love with me.

Journal Entry

December 2, 2013

So here's what happens with Chelsea. Everything's fine until I get drunk, black out, and accuse her of a bunch of shit that I don't remember. Now, on Monday, I don't even remember why I bailed on her Saturday for dinner. This all comes down to and can be solved by one thing: not drinking. If I didn't drink, then I wouldn't be calling her and texting her. I wouldn't be obsessing about her and Mason. I am creating all of the self-imposed drama because of how much I'm drinking. It shouldn't matter, it's all a game, and there is no end game. We all make mistakes, and it's time to admit to this one. Drinking is the cause, and I'm taking Chelsea down. I just need to stop being a fucking dick and doing stupid shit when I drink. My tolerance is through the roof right now. I've had a hard time not drinking.

Just stop with Chelsea. Don't seek her out, and stop making future plans with her. Remember, the girls in the pile took something from you, attention, and gave nothing back to you, and it hurt. Stop repeating the same fucking pattern, with drinking and girls, over and over. Isn't this getting old, asshole?

Mason—short, ugly, ghetto punk, ghetto car, dead-end job, ass-hole. If Chelsea wants to be with him, then there's nothing you can do. Every time you see them talking or hanging out, just laugh. Good for her if she's into him and the attention that he gives her. She'll figure it out eventually, or she'll wind up marrying the troll who wooed her with some bullshit Michael Kors watch for Christmas. God, why the fuck do I know all of this? I'm my own worst enemy.

Having Chelsea in my life, coupled with excessive drinking, was beginning to take me down. I would find myself drinking over her every single night. Any time she reached out to me, it either made my day or broke my heart. My ego, my pride, my confidence—that package that I carry with me everywhere was affected by her every single day. In many ways, Chelsea became another addiction. I had become so fucking obsessed about the fact that she was dating a total fucking loser.

Journal Entry

December 20, 2013

Mason and Chelsea. It has to be put to bed. I was informed that something happened between them, something not good, and now I'm carrying the burden of being one of the only people who know. Last week, she was at my place and didn't say one good thing about him. The question I ask is why all of this matters? I care for her, but I can't keep playing the game of being Peter Pan, swooping down and saving the day. I put myself in this position; she didn't ask for it! Just like several other relationships in my past, I'm trying to fix her.

When she is not getting attention from Mason, she comes to me. That's it. I cannot control what she does, and I cannot control him. What I do have power over is myself and to not involve myself with any of it. It ultimately gets me nowhere. Yes, I'm self-conscious around Mason, I admit it, and I know it's fucking ridiculous. It's a matter of my own self-confidence, not this fucking troll mother-fucker. You're getting used, dude, smarten the fuck up.

Soon thereafter, I went to New York City for New Year's Eve. As usual, it was fucking mayhem: total debauchery for two straight days. During that trip, I was carrying the stress of having Chelsea in my life, for better or for worse. Our friendship was crippling me, and my ability to act in a responsible manner evaporated. I didn't know how much longer I could last behaving like this. Drinking, the pile, depression, and anxiety. Its buildup was becoming my Achilles' heel. I felt like some sort of end was creeping in.

Journal Entry

January 2, 2014

7:00 a.m.—In Newark airport this morning, filled with anxiety. I just got the bartender to serve me four shots of Crown for breakfast. I'm currently sipping on a Coors Light to wash them down. Hey, dumbass, the anxiety might have something to do with the last month and half of fucking up and the debauchery that you've put yourself through. They're all factors, and I'm paying for it. What about trying to eliminate drinking again, just for a month, so that you can get some normalcy and fitness back in your life? Can you do it?

Ask yourself: How are you going to get back your confidence and swagger? Step one, stop drinking. Step two, get fit. End of story.

Pick up your guitar again, find another hobby that can be a creative outlet, read more, go to Portland on weekends, try new things, try new foods, engage more with your running team and cycling team, find another group of friends, fly under the radar, quit Facebook, surround yourself with good peeps. Train more in Bend, look for new jobs, buy some new clothes, and stop doing cocaine, for fuck's sake. Set higher standards. You're not your other friends. You're you; act like you! The party is over, motherfucker. Time to focus on making good decisions.

After returning from the East Coast, while driving home from the Portland airport, I became more motivated than ever to start figuring out my life from the beginning. I knew what was holding me back. I knew I had to stop drinking, to stop surrounding myself with people who brought me down. I needed to start making good decisions. It was becoming more obvious that Chelsea was not going to budge from Mason. Finally, their relationship had progressed enough that they had moved in together. For fuck's sake, I drank a shitload when I heard that—probably texted her a bunch of accusatory shit as well. In fact, I'm sure of it. I fucking hated it. All of it. Meanwhile, I was at my wits end with the hangovers, the depression, the anxiety, the anger, and the self-degradation.

The invincibility that I had been manufacturing for myself was dying. My life had been unraveling right before my eyes. I needed to take action for myself, assume some responsibility. As I turned off of I-5 toward Corvallis, I had a plan and a reason. I wanted more out of life, and I knew there were things that I needed to replace. The motivation was oozing out of my eyes and ears; I could feel purpose. I was on a rampage to step out of the shadows and away from other people's expectations of me and to truly start kicking ass. But wait.

While picking up some snacks in the Shell gas station right off of the interstate on the final push back home to Corvallis, the six-packs of IPAs caught my eye in the back of the store. They looked so inviting, so tempting. Maybe I could just have one more night of drinking before I tackled life. It's not going to hurt anything, right? Plus, I've got some big plans, so I deserve it. I have my plan of action, so why can't I just start tomorrow?

After an hour-long detour, I arrived at my apartment drunk as fuck. In just sixty minutes, I had chugged a dozen beers as if they were water. I fell out of my car and crawled up to my apartment to pass out on the floor. Just like with other past binges, it was amazing that I didn't kill myself when I was driving. Pitying myself that I couldn't stick to my plan for a single evening, I launched into yet another bender for the ages. I consciously started to break myself, physically, emotionally, and mentally. I embraced the pain, the depression, and the anguish as though I had a chip on my shoulder about everything that had ever happened to me—ever. I was the victim of everyone else's bad habits. It was no longer about having a good time; my life was about getting as fucked up as possible, as much as possible, without regard to myself or anyone else. I was convinced that I could live the rest of my life like this, in a complete fucking lie.

After six weeks of relentless drinking, along with total physical and mental self-destruction, a snowstorm rolled into Corvallis.

CHAPTER 19

Four years into sobriety, I am amazed that I'm still alive. This morning, Brian texted me, simply saying, "Happy sober day, homie." Since the day I got sober, February 11, 2014, Brian has sent the same exact text on the eleventh of each month. The gesture means the world to me. Brian helps me in the process of maintaining my sobriety. Yet he's not the only friend who offers steadfast support. Overwhelming support has been offered by so many people, both new and old friends, through the good times and through the dark times.

At first, I was going to end this book by describing the day I got sober, recounting the details, from the best of my memory, of my life leading up to February 11, 2014, and nothing beyond that date. The idea stemmed from Moby's memoir, *Porcelain*, which I was reading around the time I started writing. His memoir culminated at the apex of his career, when he released his multiplatinum album *Play*. If I had followed through with that original plan, though, I would have disregarded the process that has kept me alive over the last few years since getting sober. I'm tired of emulating what other people have done. I want this book to be written by me, with my style, in my own personal way, with my voice. This is a departure from how I have lived most of my life emulating others.

This past weekend, I had the chance to catch up with one of my former teammates on the St. Lawrence ski team, my friend Hattie, who was visiting Portland from her home in Alaska. She was in town for a conference. We had not seen each other in quite some time. Hattie largely knew me only as a skier and fellow adventurer; she was a regular participant on our yearly pilgramage to Bend in between our semesters at college. Hattie mainly only knew of the innocent and caring side of me. I asked her if she would read the chapter in this book dedicated to SLU. She agreed. One of my goals in having her read the accounts of my dark college years was to see if she saw any hints of my destructive nature throughout our time during college. After reading the excerpt, she calmly said that she had no idea that I had another, more sinister side. Hattie's comment only served to reinforce the idea that very few people knew the whole story. It reminded me of the pride that I used to feel when I was drinking: the pride that I could hide all of my secrets, aided by the capacity to be a social chameleon. Ultimately, that pride almost destroyed me.

It's extremely important for me to note that my years of partying were not all bad. Look, I had some fucking awesome times and met some terrific people. I don't regret most of the experiences. Would I do it all over again? That's impossible to say. However, I will say that I am grateful to have gone through the whole ordeal mostly without serious injury. The fact that I did not do permanent damage to myself does not make any sense. By being sober, I actually have the opportunity to find out what I'm made of without the mask of liquor and drugs obscuring the view.

Sobriety has not come easy for me. The process, in and of itself, has been enlightening and excruciating at the same time. It's important to note that I by no means feel like I've got this sobriety thing licked. To say otherwise would be revealing my ignorance about a process that continues each and every day. As my friends in the "rooms" of twelve-step say, it's one day at a time. It took a long time for me to realize how true that reminder is.

At first, I thought sobriety simply meant just *stop drinking*. However, being sober became more than that, so much more. Since the day I stopped drinking, my life began to get better and became clearer than I ever imagined. I'm not trying to romanticize sobriety to make it sound great. There have been some crushing blows in between the times I felt good. It's through the heartache that the most impactful work on me gets done. Sustaining sobriety is not linear. Sobriety has allowed me to understand and accept some significant truths in my life, truths that I didn't even know I had the capacity to identify on my own.

My grasp of the learning began about a year into being sober. For the first year, I was just pissed off, angry, and resentful because of everything that had happened to me. *To* me. I was firmly steeped in playing the role of a victim. Fortunately, I was able to move past that mentality so that the truths I needed to confront came through.

First and foremost, I have accepted that I am an introvert. The last time that character trait showed up was at Burke Mountain Academy when I was a scared little kid. By the time I was going to St. Lawrence, I went to the ends of the earth to make sure I never felt that distress ever again—and I succeeded, for close to two decades. It was very uncomfortable for me to realize that I had to rewire my brain. While I'm not yet entirely comfortable with the adjustment, it gets easier with time.

Next to reckon with was my ego. I never thought that I had a big ego; I knew of other people with big egos, but I did not claim one. It wasn't until I paid attention to people far more aware than I was that I started to figure it out. I understand that my entire drinking career was fueled partly by my ego. I wanted to be bigger and better than everyone else. Sure, it still exists; however, I'm more conscious of how it plays into my life. I have ego checks every single day. It's a life dynamic, and by no means will I pretend otherwise.

Most recently, however, I've realized the power that my depression plays in my life. After being diagnosed in 2007, at my first visit to Sageview Psychiatric Center, I paid little respect to the severity of my depression.

Fortunately, being bipolar II was ruled out through tests. My default set-ting had been to dismiss the ups and downs as attributable to a bad day or a nasty hangover. There was even a point that I thought that I had cured my depression by improving my food intake. I thought that being vegan had cured me of the disease. What a crock of shit! Even sober, I used run-ning as a method to eradicate the depression that would wash over me occasionally. Regardless of how I tried to cure my depression by myself, I had no idea the seriousness of the role that it would play in my life. That understanding recently came to light after I hit an emotional rock bottom, resulting in another trip to the emergency room—something that had not been repeated since my second trip to Sageview in 2008. Depression, for me, is a very real disease, one that I will combat and manage for the rest of my life. Today, I accept that and will do what it takes to survive. I've strongly considered suicide before; I'd really like to avoid contemplating that in the future, whatever the cost.

⁕

Blog post:

Back to the ER...Yet Another Bottom
October 4, 2017

I checked myself into the emergency room yesterday morning. I hadn't done this since 2008, when I was drunk and suicidal. I just couldn't withstand the pain anymore, and I was desperate for help, by any means possible. I had had it with feeling like complete gar-bage, physically and mentally.

A few weeks ago, I wrote about "ten days of hell that must see the light," describing the longest depressive episode that I've expe-rienced to date. Well, those ten days turned into four weeks; the gray, the apathy, and the exhaustion have refused to go away, and it still continues to persist today. The overwhelming questions that plague me are: "Where is the final bottom?" along with "Will I feel like this forever?"

Just a few days ago, on Saturday, I had the best day I've had in longer than I can remember. For some reason, I woke up that morning feeling a respite from the stranglehold that depression had on me. I was up in Portland, clowning around with a friend, and everything seemed good to go. I felt "normal," whatever that means these days. However, during the day's run, I tweaked my hip. At the time it didn't feel like a terribly big deal, and I largely brushed it off. But on Sunday, it was a different story. My hip had tightened up overnight, and I was in pain.

On its own, a relatively benign injury, as was the case, is easy to manage. However, due to my elevated emotional instability and depressive state, the injury seemed like the end of the world. While on the phone with a Brian early Sunday morning, I just crumbled. I pleaded with him: "When the hell is this shit going to end? When are these fucking setbacks going to stop? I'm so fucking sick of this!" From that point on, the good vibes I had going the previous day all but disappeared. By Sunday afternoon, I was back in bed with the shades drawn, unable to move, wrought with the overwhelming feeling that everything was crumbling down once again.

Monday came—same thing. My hip was beginning to feel better, but its impact had set off another spell of oppressive frustration, hopelessness, and, once again, pure apathy. Then, I woke up yesterday and succumbed to the tension in my head, the anxiety in my chest, and the relentless feelings of helplessness. I needed more help.

My experience in the ER yesterday was not a good one. For the first time in my life, I played direct witness as to how some ER's handle mental health issues. Without going into the details of the experience, let's just say I left in worse shape than when I arrived. After being discharged, I found myself in a fetal position, crying, lying on the cold linoleum of the hospital hallway in blue medical scrubs, pleading for help. And I didn't get it. All I wanted was to feel better.

Having gained some sort of composure after the ER experience, I scrambled to find the help I needed, visiting the local county mental health office as well as making emergency appointments with my team of psychiatrists and therapists. I was able to get in, be assessed, and come up with a game plan. I should have just gone to this group of professionals in the first place. I suppose I was in too much agony earlier in the morning to even consider that possibility.

Fortunately, I was able to gain some sort of clarity, from a physical standpoint, of what is currently going on. Blood tests taken at the ER revealed two things of significance. One, my testosterone levels had fallen well below normal again (earlier this spring I was dealing with the same thing; however, by summer I was able to recover). Two, my thyroid is out of whack.

Luckily, these two things can be fixed, to a degree, with time and patience. The mental parts of the equation will prove to be a little trickier.

After hours of professional consult and self-reflection, I have yet another game plan to address everything that is going on:

1) Take one full month off of heavy structured training (two full weeks off from running). I have not let my body rest (not counting the time off from injuries, which isn't really "time off") in well over three years. It's finally time for me to take a break and let my body fully heal on its own. If it takes

longer than a month? So be it. I don't want to go through this shit again, especially as I get older. Therefore, Rio Del Lago 100, the race I've been training for, is off the table. In 2017, I will not complete a single race that I've set out for. And that's OK, because there is a much bigger picture at stake here. I'll take my life over a race any day.

2) Focus on my creative side, which means writing and composing music. My book is still coming along well. In conjunction with that project, I am also composing a soundtrack to go along with the book. I used to sing and play the hell out of my guitar. Firing both of those passions back up will be good for the soul.

3) Just fucking chill. If I feel like binge watching *Friday Night Lights* for the second time, just do it! God, relaxation and I do not get along well. It turns out that I actually might hate the idea of relaxing. I consume myself with endless expectations, pressures, and stresses, which plays into my recent demise. I'm just fucking tired of being tired.

4) Continue to work with my trusted health professionals to dial in what I need from a medical standpoint. This part will be crucial to my recovery.

I'm hopeful that this episode will pass at some point. It has to! Yet the last month has offered nothing to the contrary. Living day to day is not working; it's more like minute to minute.

I don't wish depression, or any other chronic or perpetual disease, on anyone. For me, it's been absolute torture and hell. To try to find the silver lining of this experience has been impossible; I'm just not in a frame of mind to even consider the good that may come out of this.

Miraculously, and I really don't even understand this part, I have not had one single craving to drink throughout this entire episode. In and of itself, that is a pure fucking miracle. Perhaps that says something.

Now let's get to some of the good stuff that has come with being sober.

A few years ago, I met a woman named Betsy Hartley. We were introduced by a mutual friend who worked for Oregon State University, like Betsy does. One day, while meeting for coffee, she shared with me her incredible and unimaginable story. About six years prior, Betsy weighed four hundred pounds. The day we met, she had already lost over two hundred pounds. Let that sink in for a minute: two hundred fucking pounds! And she had done it mostly on her own. After hearing her story of a U-turn lifestyle change, I could immediately relate. Not yet sober when we met, I knew the end of my drinking days were fast approaching. Knowing that she was successfully combating obesity, as well as type-2 diabetes, inspired me.

A year later, after our first meeting, Betsy and I decided to go into business together. Our company, Novo Veritas, LLC, focuses on helping people believe that they, too, can tackle significant lifestyle changes if they truly want it. We assist people with reaching their goals by providing support, community, and accountability. A couple of years into the venture, we both feel that we are now truly getting started with our mission to help change the world. It's a very important project for me to be involved with because our business helps keep me accountable each and every day. To top it off, Betsy and I get to see some major life changes occur in others. In fact, we're working with a woman who is experiencing triple-digit weight loss, along with a massive resurgence of self-confidence. Needless to say, the work we do to help others is incredibly fulfilling. And as for Betsy's transformation? Last year, she completed her first hundred-mile trail race. From four hundred pounds to an ultra-runner. Can you say "Fuck yeah!"

Betsy and I, the Novo Veritas team, outside of the Whiteside Theater in Corvallis, OR, moments before one of our first public speaking presentations, 2016

Some people in recovery say that when you get sober, you find out who your friends are pretty quickly. I like to think of it as the other way around. Yes, I lost some friends when I stopped drinking, but as time passed, I realized that the people who stopped staying in touch weren't really friends at the outset. However, along with Betsy, my friends and mentors in recovery, the ultra-running community, and countless other quality people whom I've met over the past few years, I found that I've gained more friends rather than lost them.

Blog post:

Friendships Lost and Gained in Sobriety

I used to love to party. I loved the thrill of getting together with friends and taking that initial celebratory shot in anticipation of what the night together could bring: shenanigans, transgressions, and good ol' chaos. Toward the end of the dark days of my partying, there were several friends whom I relied on and used as crutches to help feed my addictive nature. Those involved had no idea of what was going on in my head at the time.

In the past, I have prided myself on the company I kept and the vast number of friends whom I spent time with; even the number of Facebook friends I maintained was crucial to my identity. Being the gregarious extrovert that I was back then, it was easy to maintain a facade on the outside that I liked everyone, for fear of being lonely. Now, almost three years into this journey of sobriety, I am indeed still finding out what genuine and authentic friends mean, friends whom I can rely on without agenda in both the good and bad times.

One thing I noticed when I first got sober is that I began to have fewer text messages and phone calls coming in. At that point I figured it was because no one wanted to hang out with the sober guy and therefore be at risk to potentially encourage and/or witness a relapse. It was a terrifying feeling to know that people were putting distance between themselves and me. Maybe people just didn't know how to react or what to say? Today, I get that it must have been hard to know how to react when one of your friends comes out with this secret that he's been hiding for years.

In the meantime, in recovery, I still found it very uncomfortable to open myself to others who were also attempting sobriety. That first year of sobriety I was lost, not able to decipher who my friends were and who had my back. At that point, I was still in a very egotistical frame of mind, thinking the world still revolved around me, that everyone should take my feelings into consideration. Truth be told, everyone has their own shit going on. It's not just me. Many people indicated they indeed had my back, even the acquaintances from my partying days, but it just didn't feel authentic at the time. I found myself wanting to isolate, and I was unwilling to understand who really cared for my wellbeing. Today, I can clearly see that the majority of friends I kept even during those dark times are very much still in support of what I'm trying to do with sobriety. It would have been a mistake to give up on those friendships.

I can think of a few old friends in particular whom I used to party hard and hang with all of the time. The last time I heard from these people was when I was on a text message parade during the last weekend of drinking in February 2014, having locked myself inside, alone, to effectively drink as much as possible and reach my bottom. Neither I nor they have reached out once since that weekend. It used to confuse me why this was the case. Now I ask: Were those people really worth investing time and energy into anyway?

As recovery continued, the distance between many friends still grew. Hell, even today there are several people in my life who have just become as distant as can be for whatever the reason. Perhaps they are dealing with their own circumstances, perhaps not. Again, I know it's not all about me, but it's just sad to realize that some of the close friends I had in the past have more or less vanished. This certainly begs the question: Did these relationships truly have any other meaning and substance than just the commonality of partying? Who really knows? Today, with a more lucid understanding of what true friendship means, I am finding that it is certainly about quality rather than quantity.

The people whom I rely on today as friends and mentors are simply amazing. I cannot believe the quality of their characters and the conversation that I can have with each of these folks. My only challenge is to continue to keep contact, as I can very easily get lost in my own thoughts and rituals. If I go long enough without contact, then the undeniable feeling of loneliness walks in.

This isn't intended to be a cry for attention on my end. The reason that I bring this to the table is that I have run into a few people lately who are new to sobriety, and their "friends" pertain to their heartache and sadness. I can see the pain on their faces and in their eyes about how they seem to be "losing" friends. While that may be the case, I wish I could paint a picture to assure all of them that they are not alone and that many new friends are waiting around the corner. For me, meeting friends in recovery happened over time, not all at once. I had to take care of my own shit before feeling comfortable reaching out to new people. This is still a challenge today.

Generally, I enjoy being around people. However, I also enjoy being alone. Not lonely but alone. Being on my own allows me to refuel spiritually, mentally, and physically. In no way do I shut myself off from meeting anyone new; it just takes a little longer for me to grow comfortable with each new respective relationship.

For the newcomer to sobriety: this process, not just with friends, but with every facet of life, gets easier. As a friend of mine said last night, "Don't stop before the miracle happens.

Next comes the sport of ultra-running. Simply put, I fucking love it.

In September 2016, I completed and achieved an overall top-ten placing in my first hundred-mile trail race, the Pine to Palm 100, held each year in the rugged Siskiyou Mountains of southern Oregon. Completing that race sealed my love for the sport. Dating back to my teenage years, when competing as a junior cross-country ski racer, I always had a dream to be an elite, maybe even professional, endurance athlete. The appeal of living the lifestyle of a professional athlete was tempting and constantly on my mind.

Unfortunately, those dreams were never realized in skiing. Then, when I was a cyclist, drinking and partying largely interrupted chasing down any big athletic dreams.

Moments after completing my first one-hundred mile
trail running race, Pine to Palm 100, 2016

As I enter my seventh year as an ultra-runner, at the ripe old age of thirty-eight, I am finally able to say that I am pursuing that dream of living and racing like a pro, with a fierce and full-on vengeance. This would never have happened if I were still drinking. Even though it took over twenty years to get to this point, I don't feel like I'm too old for the challenge. I am grateful I can embrace the lifestyle of full-time training. Regardless of any results that I may or may not achieve, I am literally living a dream, striving to be the best version of myself that I can be. I even have a couple of sponsors to help support the endeavor! It's pretty fucking awesome.

My idea of a healthy and viable relationship with women has also changed quite dramatically. The "pile" of girls that I surrounded myself with during my darkest days of partying served as one more kind of addiction. I was so blinded by obsessive thinking and substance abuse that I lost sight of what a real, authentic, and honest relationship was. In all fairness, I have maintained communication with a couple of girls in the pile, mainly because we shared so much time together. However, I am no longer bound to them by obsession in any way. Furthermore, in sobriety, I have met some fantastic women who are attracted to me for who I am today, not to some crazy identity that I cast out to the world for decades. I am now capable of trusting my instincts to avoid toxic and meaningless relationships. The time for those is over.

Blog post:

"You're All I Ever Wanted"

I've been lucky to be in some tremendous relationships in my life. To this day, I remain close with many of the women I've dated throughout my life. In fact, someone I dated during my first years at St. Lawrence University continues to be one of my best friends, even though we don't see each other very often. For me, the relationships I've had, for the most part, have been very important and meaningful. Even though the relationship part of some equations didn't work out, I still value the bond of the friendships that developed. I wish I could say that was true for all of my past relationships, but unfortunately I cannot. Today I accept that.

I've also been lucky to go through some less-than-ideal relationships. I say "lucky" because through those relationships, I learned an awful lot about myself and what the opposite sex means to me. As many of you know, I was engaged to be married at one time in my life. For the better, and for both parties, it didn't work out. In fact, it was brought to my attention that just nine months before I was to be married, I caught wind that most of my friends were planning to boycott the wedding. Needless to say, it was a dark period in my life, but today I am all the better for having experienced that time.

In recovery, they say that it's best not to date anyone during the first year. Looking back on this advice, almost three years into this journey of sobriety, I see that it is indeed sound advice. During the last couple of years of my partying days, I was drawn to women who I knew would help feed my addiction to alcohol. I felt safe around them because I knew that I would not be judged for all of the destruction I was doing to myself. It got so bad that I used to daydream, with one person in particular, that she and I would lock ourselves in my apartment for a weekend and have an all-out drug-and-alcohol-induced bender. It was dark, but at the time, I didn't know any better. "Lucky" for me, toward the end of my drinking streak, my daydream came true with that person, and one weekend we did exactly what I had wanted. It was a true act of selfishness.

When I got sober, I more or less took two years off from truly pursuing any relationships. At that point, I did not trust myself to make the right decision about whom I should spend time with. I had become trapped in thinking that a certain kind of woman was right for me. Clearly, based on my recent track record during the last few years of partying, I was headed down the same road that I had found myself on back in 2006 when I made the decision to propose to someone. I needed those first two years in recovery to take a good, hard look at the women I surrounded myself with and to feel comfortable with myself. Luckily, I once again began to start trusting myself and finally encouraged myself to be open to the idea of letting someone in.

*I wrote Appetite for Addiction over a year in one place,
Coffee Culture in Corvallis, OR. Together with the gals that
kept me properly caffeinated during the process, 2018*

My first relationship in sobriety was great. To this day, I still con-sider her a good friend. Even though the relationship didn't work out, we still share many of the same passions and interests. I see her at races from time to time, and we both enjoy catching up with each other. There are no hard feelings; we had said what was on our minds, and we moved forward as friends. I know this can be a rare occurrence, so I am grateful to still have this friendship.

Today, now that I am gaining more and more clarity about what I would look for in a partner, everything seems simpler, much like it did when I first started dating back in middle school. I remember the innocence of that relationship. Her name was Sarah, and we played trombone together in jazz band. Holding hands at recess was a big deal for both of us back then. Does that innocence have to be lost?

Even though I'm still guarded in some ways, I feel like I have a better sense of who that person might be. Now, I know that all I ever wanted was a partner, a lover, and a best friend looking to share the best of life's experiences together. Someone who is passionate about life—not about running, necessarily, but about something that fills her heart to the fullest. Passion is one of the sexiest things I can think of.

It's taken a while to realize this, but the difference this time around is that I don't feel the need to push the issue. I don't feel the need to be in a relationship just for the sake of being in a relationship. I've done that before, and it wasn't the best way to approach it. To me, when it happens, if it happens, I hope that it can come in a natural and organic way, just like it did with Sarah way back when at Gateway Middle School.

⁓

This book isn't about Sarah, or Lisa, or Kristin, or Hannah, or Chelsea, or even Lauren for that matter. Yes, in some cases I had some bad shit happen to me, and they all played their parts in this story to a great degree. However, I take responsibility for my role in each of these relationships, because let's face it, I wasn't necessarily in the right frame of mind either. I had my moments of being crazy, obsessive, and belligerent. I own it. Maybe it's time for me to let all of that shit go. Things change, people change, I change.

Alcoholism, addiction, depression, and suicide. All of these topics on their own can be incredibly stigmatic. But together? They can be downright lethal, as they almost were to me. My hope is that by continuing to talk about them, in an open and public forum, I will encourage others to do the same. Simply based on the support and feedback that I've privately received, it's been astonishing for me to understand, in my tiny little circle alone, how many people are suffering silently. The stigma that we, as a human race, bring to these dangerous subjects is not fair—not to family, to friends, to loved ones, to coworkers, or to whomever. It's just not fair. No one really knows what happens behind closed doors, and no one really knows what people suffer from in isolation. And to assume that we do? That's just insanity.

"So why do you think you're feeling so lonely?" Karen asked.

"I don't know. I think it probably has to do with my depression and anxiety...probably stems from something to do with my childhood," I replied.

"OK, so what does that actually mean?" she asked.

"That my relationship with my mom has something to do with it," I said.

"Why don't you try something other than telling yourself the same story that you've always told yourself. Doesn't it get old for you to keep telling yourself the same damn narrative that never seemed to work in the first place?"

"Huh?" I asked.

After a few thoughtful moments, her comment struck home for me: maybe I have been telling myself the same story *about* myself, in various ways, for the better part of thirty-eight years. I've lived with a narrative, some illusion, based on very little factual evidence, which has become my own worst enemy. My mind has tended to wander off down the rabbit hole of dwelling on the past and living in the future. The rewiring of certain thought patterns, with Karen's help and guidance, has been a very profound experience as I continue to respect the fact that I am, indeed, an alcoholic. Diving in to psychotherapy has been crucial to my sustained recovery. Karen is my therapist and a lifeline. We have been working together for over three years, basically since I got sober.

Maybe I don't have to be the victim of having a depressed mother when I was growing up. Maybe I have the power to change the relentless narrative that streams through my mind every single day: I'm unattractive, unlikeable, overweight, never good enough, and unworthy of achieving my goals. Constant reassurance has been a crutch that I've leaned on for years. Maybe everything that I've been telling myself for as long as I can remember is an illusion, a fabrication of others' expectations and opinions.

My response echoed the way my mind had just been blown.

Then Karen posed the simplest of questions: "Can we move on now?"

Looking forward into the unknown, Grand Canyon, 2017

Acknowledgments

To my parents, Lyn Horton and John Newell: thank you for bringing me into this world and supporting me as I chase down my dreams.

To my lifelong best friends and older brothers, Matt Molyneux and Matt Whitcomb: long live M2S and the adventures that will happen for us together in the future.

To a few of the best friends a guy could have who helped me keep my head high when times were low, Brian Hetzel, Ben Hicks, and Jeff Costello (number ten): you boys have been a very important and influential source of unwavering support.

To my mentors, Ed Hamel, Davis Smith, Michael Larsen, Randy Perkins, and Ian Torrence: you are the guys who helped shape me into who I am today.

To Betsy Hartley: The adventure has only started. We've got some important shit to do. Let's do this! FY!

To Jason Lemieux: thank you for helping me create a competitive edge for myself and for staying in touch.

To Kieran Pinney, Jon Kaplan, Buffy Hastings, Dan Marchetti, Brett Harvey, and Uncle E., some of the best college friends a guy could ask for: I am so grateful to have kept our relationships strong today.

To the girls at the SLU Delta Delta Delta house: you all have been incredibly supportive, both publicly and privately, while I share my personal stories in a public forum. Thank you!

To my teammates on the St. Lawrence ski team, Eric Pepper, Hattie Shelton, Z-free, Andrew Wadowski, Dustin Williamson, Brent Freeman, and Brenna Knowles: you all played a role in my keeping some semblance of innocence at college.

To Hillary Baker-Sunderland: to continue having you in my life means the world.

To my ski teammates and coaches at Burke Mountain Academy: Jen Douglas, James Upham, Jordan Manges, Erin Wheeler, Jen Dalley, and Forrest Janukajtis: Thank you for keeping me going, even if you didn't know it at the time.

To my Bend cycling buddies Rob Angelo, Tim Jones, TJ, and Agent Legs: thank you all for keeping me on track by making sure I got my ass to team rides, especially when it hurt to get out of bed.

To Annie Mac: thank you for believing in me when I didn't believe in myself.

To Jade: Thank you for letting me help you through the toughest transition in your life. I love my little sister!

To Patrick Means: thank you for being real, authentic, and one of the most bad-ass dudes I know.

To Andrew Miller, one of my favorite running partners: let the adventures continue!

To Coach Gottlieb: Thank you for being a trustworthy friend; I'm always up for some miles with you and Ace. Go Beavs!

To Coach Tinkle: Thank you for asking me if I'm trying to be the best ever or the best that I can be.

To Mariva England: I hope that we will always make it a point to stay in touch.

To Toby H., Randy J., Shannon J., Ryan I., Sarah D., Maren V., Louise B., and all of my friends in the Corvallis "rooms": you helped me to make sense of sobriety.

To David Gerkman, Amber Spain, and Kaitlynn Phillips: We made a great team. Thank you for your unwavering support through one of the toughest years of my life.

To my social media consultation team Brecklin Milton and Addie Howell: thank you for showing this old guy some new tricks.

To Cindy Aron: thank you for asking me to finally move on.

To my editing team Lyn Horton and Kerri Chavez: thank you for your insight and help with tightening up my story!

To the authors who helped give me the courage to share my story of sobriety in an open forum: Rich Roll, Mishka Shubaly, Khalil Rafati, and David Clark.

And last but not least, to Emery: Who saved whom?

Fiction

The Man on the Moor (2004)
Olga and David (2014)
Elmore Sounds (2015)

Plays

The Man on the Moor (2015)
A Mere Passing Shadow (2015)

Made in the USA
Lexington, KY
17 June 2015